animal days

Published by Bay Books Pty Ltd.
61-69 Anzac Parade, Kensington
NSW 2033 Australia
©1984 Bay Books
Designed by Sackville Design Group Ltd.
National Library of Australia
Card Number & ISBN 0 85835 529 9
All rights reserved.
Printed in Singapore
by Toppan Printing Company

animal days

David Sharp

Edited by
Cathy Kilpatrick B.Sc., Dip.Ed., F.Z.S.

Bay Books

Contents

Introduction	9
The crocodile	10
The salmon	30
The oyster	48
The albatross	58
The hammerhead shark	70
The pelican	82
The dragonfly	92
The whale	104
The octopus	118

Introduction

The lives of most wild animals are mysterious to man and none is completely understood by even the most knowledgeable expert. However, enough is known to stimulate our curiosity and make us ask such questions as: 'How do animals spend their days?' and 'What would it be like to be a whale, dragonfly or a crocodile?' A closer look at a few of the world's most interesting creatures, described in this book, may help to answer these questions.

In a world of shrinking animal resources, which is suffering the gradual erosion of its genetic treasures, curiosity about wildlife and concern for its future are more important than ever before. The animal kingdom is confronting great dangers while, paradoxically, receiving more scientific attention and interest from conservation groups than in the past. By attempting to understand each animal's behaviour, physical attributes and how it adapts to its particular environment, we can help to protect our wildlife and to conserve the most endangered species which are threatened with imminent extinction.

One of the areas most threatened is the watery environment of the oceans, seas and rivers, which cover nearly three-quarters of the world's surface. It was here in the warm coastal waters of the oceans that life began and the long evolutionary thread started to unwind. Now their rich and varied wildlife are threatened by over-fishing, and chemical and industrial pollution. Animals have adapted in wonderful ways to their marine habitat, their physiology changing to meet the environment's challenges, but the fate of many animal species and communities now hangs in the balance as some nations fail to observe international agreements on whaling, and salmon streams are poisoned by chemical pollutants and industrial waste. The evolutionary balance, maintained by nature for many centuries, is being gradually eroded, and severe damage to one animal species may affect the health of the whole marine community.

This book focuses on nine animals, describing a single day in the life of each animal followed by relevant information and scientific data. The day outlined may be unusual or typical as the animal experiences birth, death, flight from a predator or just its routine feeding and hunting in order to survive.

Of course, none of the animals described experiences the full range of its activities in one day, but the day described does offer a characteristic sample of its adventures. In one story an octopus fights with a dangerous Moray eel, in another a salmon makes the spawning run up-river to its natal stream to breed. By exploring the animal world in this way, we can understand these beautiful creatures better and see the world through their eyes.

The Crocodile

Patches of lily pods swayed lazily as low, log-like shapes silently floated past them towards the gently sloping beach. A lily trotter skittered on enormous spidery feet across the broad pads well away from the large green eyes that glided slowly by. The creek was still quiet with the surprise of morning as the crocodiles clambered out of the water into the sunshine.

Weeds clung to their plated backs in patches, camouflaging the regular pattern of their armoured skins. Seven ponderous shapes moved heavily up the loamy margin of the creek towards a fringe of low bushes which overhung a bank and settled with grunts to bask in the warming air. Their eyes blinked slowly as they surveyed the beach with its shallow backwater and the great lake sprinkled with low islands which lay beyond. The tall papyrus reeds swayed their tufted heads rhythmically. None of it had changed much since the crocodiles' ancestors had first made the beach their home, long before the men in the broad valley nearby had learned to stand upright on two legs.

Out beyond the lily pads and the water cabbage, the water swirled as a powerful tail swept the biggest crocodile onto a new tack. Slowly, he swam back along his beat; eighty metres, turn, eighty metres, turn. It was a patrol as regular as a pendulum. His jade-green eyes, their pupils narrowed to vertical slits against the sun's reflection on the water, observed the creek with concentration. The tip of his snout rose clear of the ripples that shuddered across the smooth surface of the lake. When he turned, the ripples broke lightly against his slight bow wave, and the skin about his gnarled snout closed delicately to cover his nostrils for a moment. There was no sound or smell or moving thing to alarm him. His stomach was comfortable, neither full nor empty of food, but somewhere at the back of his brain a thread of experience signalled that he must be ready to guard his possessions – the female crocodiles – that were now warming up nicely on the shore.

Three of the four females on the beach were mature. One, smaller than the others, had yet to lay her first eggs, but a week ago one of the mature females had stayed on shore all night while the other crocodiles went out on the lake. She had chosen a spot about six metres from the bank, on the landward side, and scraped a hole. Taking a great bite out of the topsoil, she had spat it to one side, then scraped more soil away with her forefeet. She had removed thick pieces of roots by grasping them cleverly with her feet and pushing them to one side. The earth she pushed backwards and then brought her hindfeet into play to shovel the soil clear of the hole, she then settled over the hole.

The night had been a quiet one. The night noises she heard were mostly distant, but she was alert to the small sounds near her. Her flanks had stretched and flexed as she deposited her eggs, one after another, in the shallow pit. As each egg rolled down the side of the nest, she had gathered a clod of earth with one of her forefeet and carefully scooped it into the pit to cover the egg. When she had finished, each egg was surrounded with enough loose earth to prevent it breaking against the shell of the neighbouring one. At the end of the night, she had laid 32 eggs, which lay in three layers in the pit. She had shovelled the remaining loose earth into the hole and rolled it flat by carefully pressing it down with the smooth scales of her

Opposite page:
This crocodile is surfacing under a fish eagle, whose reflection is visible in the water below. Crocodiles usually float low in the water with only the nostrils and eyes above the surface. In their stomachs they may carry several kilos of stones which have the effect of stabilising their bodies in the water. Thus they balance the buoyant lungs as they lie below the crocodile's centre of gravity.

When several crocodiles are grouped together, as here in a muddy pool, their bodies appear to merge into each other, providing an example of disruptive colouration. They are cold-blooded creatures that cannot, unlike birds and mammals, maintain their body temperatures within certain limits. Instead, their temperature tends to be similar to that of its surroundings to within a few degrees. Thus it cannot sweat to keep cool in intense heat or shiver to retain warmth in cold conditions. However, crocodiles have evolved a routine to suit their environment. Thus they escape the extreme heat of the day by lying in the shade or the water and bask in the weaker sunshine in the early morning and evening. At night, they often return to the water to conserve their body heat.

These Nile crocodiles are mating in some swampy water. Prior to mating, the male thrashes the water with his snout and tail, displaying himself to the female. Mating always takes place during the dry season and about 90 eggs are laid as a result and are placed in shallow pits constructed near the water's edge in the shade of trees and bushes. The female crocodile stands guard over the nest and its precious eggs until the young start to grunt softly inside the shells at about 12 weeks. The young hatch during the rainy season when insects, their main food, are abundant.

belly. After giving it a final sweep with her tail, she inspected the result to make sure that the nest site was well camouflaged. Since that day, she had spent most of her time in the shade of a nearby ambach bush, ready to rush to the defence of her eggs.

None of the three males on the narrow beach was mature. They were little more than two-and-a-half metres long, all much alike in appearance, except one who had about ten centimetres of his tail missing. He had lost it early in his life when a large turtle had snapped at him, shortening his two metres of length. He had escaped into the burrow he had made in the river bank. The wound had healed and his health had not suffered once the shock had worn off.

Further along the arm of the beach, the dark shapes of another group of crocodiles lay on the cracked mud. In the water before them, their most vigorous male patrolled up to the edge of his neighbour's territory. Each male turned punctiliously away from the other, never crossing the invisible line that marked the limit of his base. A new male lay at the tip of the small headland that marked the end of the shelving shoreline. He was a little over three metres long, younger and slimmer than the patrolling males.

For some hours he had watched the patrollers and looked across towards the two groups of sunbathers. Slowly, he paddled himself forwards, slithering on the polished scales of his pale belly until the water buoyed him up. He circled past the first male, who paused to watch him carefully. The young crocodile curved in towards the second male's beach. He was swimming well, his body low in the water. The stones in his stomach, gathered after a long search up a river that fed the great lake, held him at an angle to the surface so that only the top of his head showed above the water. The stones

These young crocodiles (top) are resting in the water with only their eyes and nostrils in view above the surface. These are located on small humps above the level of the long, flat snout to allow vision and respiration when the crocodile's body is submerged. Unlike other reptiles, the ears are protected by a special flap of skin which prevents the water entering them.

The crocodile's powerful jaws are armed with simple, conical and socketed teeth of various sizes. New teeth grow throughout the animal's life, gradually pushing the old ones up out of their cavities. The tongue is implanted firmly in the mouth and cannot be extended beyond the snout. Inside the mouth a flap of skin separates the internal nostrils from the mouth cavity. This ingenious arrangement allows the crocodile to breathe when the snout is under water.

Found all over Africa south of the Sahara, the Nile crocodile is the most familiar species of the true crocodiles. It is easily distinguished by its long, broad snout and it measures up to six metres in length. However, once it was not uncommon to find crocodiles up to 10m long. This Nile crocodile is stepping into the water. It is a strong swimmer, the tail only being used for propulsion. It swishes from side to side, propelling the creature through the water, while the legs are drawn in close to the body. Crocodiles usually take to the water in intense heat and to kill prey.

weighed about three kilogrammes. It was after swallowing the last of them that he had turned again towards the lake and swum the 270km back to his native waters.

The big four-and-a-half-metre male continued his patrol, always pausing in the same spot for six or seven minutes before resuming his slow swim. He snuffled the air, and at 30m he spotted the intruder. The newcomer changed course slightly to curl past the guarding male, but when only 20m separated them, the water foamed around the bigger male. His head rose from the water and he sent a thunderous, challenging bellow across the water. The pair of crocodiles faced one another, almost stationary. Their tails arched out of the water to crash down at the same moment, as the breath hissed from their mouths and the pair of scent-producing glands under their necks squirted out a fine spray of musk-smelling liquid.

Unseen by either of the antagonists, the patrolling male from further up the beach swam rapidly towards his neighbour's group. He climbed onto the land and walked, with his body well clear of the ground, towards one of the females. His high-stepping walk covered the ground quickly, and he was soon nuzzling her gently, stroking the secretion of his neck glands onto the back of her neck.

Fifty metres away, the young crocodile held his ground for a while. The older reptile began to clash his great jaws together. With a surge of his tail, he shot forwards, lifting himself partly out of the water, and charged. The younger crocodile turned with a nimbleness that saved him easily but decided that he had taken on more than he could safely handle. He swam rapidly out to open water with his snout held high, clear of the water. His pursuer made a fearful sight. He swam half out of the water, slapping it with his tail, smashing his great teeth together and roaring out a challenge which could be heard a kilometre away. The chase slowed down after 100m and the older crocodile bellowed loudly again as he swam backwards for a few metres. Then he turned to shore, leaving the defeated youngster to swim for the point of the headland.

This swamp crocodile is emerging from the water with a snake in its jaws. A native of India, Sri Lanka and Burma, the swamp crocodile has a shorter snout than that of the Nile species and the scutes on its back are not arranged in so regular a pattern. The long jaws of the crocodile contain a formidable array of both conical and socketed teeth for tearing the flesh of its prey. Its eyes are positioned high on its head so that the reptile can submerge almost totally without its breathing or sight being affected by the water.

This swamp, or mugger, crocodile is feeding on an elephant carcass in Sri Lanka. Crocodiles generally feed on waterfowl and wading birds, fish and small mammals. They lie in wait for their unsuspecting victims near waterholes and game trials, taking their prey by surprise and dragging it into the water to drown it. Sometimes the prey is knocked out or killed by a powerful blow from the crocodile's tail or head. Once killed, the prey is dragged by the crocodile on to the bank and dismembered. Sometimes it is hidden in a cavity or pit for several days before being eaten.

The water was warming up as the sun rose higher in the sky. There were still a couple of hours to go before midday and the water around him was 30°C, a temperature that inclined him to thoughts of his females on shore. As he swam towards them with unhurried dignity, still patrolling from side to side, the victor noticed that the scene on the beach was not as he had left it.

The neighbouring male was acceptable to the female who had taken his fancy. She had led him slowly into the water where they had lain, nuzzling and caressing. He had tentatively put a forefoot on her back and had found that she did not object. Gradually he hoisted himself onto her back, still stroking her with his neck. The musky smell of his glands was strong but the breeze carried it from the lake to the land. The young males rumbled uneasily. The pair of mating crocodiles twisted and turned as he wrapped his long tail around hers. They lay on their sides in the shallow water while they copulated. It was all over in little more than a minute, and they parted in time to hear the outraged bellows from the crocodile, who swam fast towards them.

The female swam lazily on a diagonal course to carry her away from the probable point of the clash between these giants. She squelched into a patch of matetite reeds and lay there half submerged in the mud. The neighbouring male took a careful look at the approaching male, uttered a half-hearted bellow, and swung himself into a high-stepping walk across the land and towards his own territory. The other crocodile gave chase, bellowing and snapping his jaws. The gap between them narrowed and the leading reptile changed his gait for a few dozen metres. He pushed off from both back legs, landed on his forefeet and repeated the manoeuvre in a series of galloping bounds rather like the running action of a rabbit

This crocodile, with its jaws open wide (bottom), is displaying a formidable array of teeth in the well-known leer. Many people find it difficult to distinguish between alligators and crocodiles as they resemble each other closely. However, whereas the teeth on the upper and lower jaws of a crocodile are aligned and engage, the alligator has a blunter jaw and the upper teeth overlap the lower ones when it closes its mouth.

or a squirrel. This carried him clear of his pursuer who paused to roar defiance at him before returning to his clan by the water.

Some of his group had taken to the water, lying in the shallows. The big male joined those on land and found a patch of shade not far from the female who was watching her nest. With a snort, he flopped down. He tilted his head back slightly so that his upper jaw opened clear of the lower one which lay comfortably on the grass. He was hot. He had no sweat glands to help in reducing his temperature so he lost some heat through evaporation from his mouth. The wide gape of his bright orange mouth was not unlike that of an enormous fledgling bird. A water dikkip landed near him and joined an Egyptian plover that had already perched on the crocodile's neck. Both birds pecked the leeches that gathered round the enormous reptile's neck and clung to the soft tissue around his teeth. The crocodile made no objection to the service that the birds performed for him, even allowing the little dikkop to pick flies off his eyelids. The dikkop soon had its fill and flew away to its own nest, built in sight of the new crocodile nest.

Throughout the middle of the day and into the afternoon the crocodiles rested, lying in the shade with their mouths propped open, sometimes slithering into shallow water for a while. It was on one of these visits to the water that the crocodile female left her nest for a few minutes. For some time the scene was peaceful enough. The grass was still in the motionless air, bleached by the sun to a uniform dun colour. The basking crocodiles did not stir at the flicker of movement on a patch of rising ground that lay inland about 30m from the nest. An olive-brown lizard darted forwards in a series of dashes, stopping as still as a stone between them. From head to tail, its body was ringed with yellow stripes. The Nile monitor had

This Nile crocodile is basking in a swamp in the heat of the African day as it cannot sweat to keep cool. It spends the night in the water to conserve its body heat which would be lost out in the air, and emerges at sunrise onto the bank where it lies in the sun, warming its body, until it becomes very hot around noon. It escapes from the hot sun by lumbering into the shade or sliding on its belly down into the water, using its legs as paddles.

understood the behaviour of the guarding female well enough and had waited for her to relinquish her post for a while. His movements were so rapid and silent that they passed unnoticed until he had begun to dig into the nest. He worked swiftly. The water dikkop returned to her nest from the lakeside nearby as the lizard uncovered the first layer of eggs. She fluttered her wings and made a commotion to arouse the dozing crocodiles to the danger.

The dominant male crocodile acted quickly, but not quickly enough to catch the predator, who made off, clutching one of the eggs in a forefoot. The monitor ran towards a rotting trunk against which he had often broken eggs to eat their contents. He scuttled over the top of the log to drop into the narrow band of shade on the other side and saw too late the bright green eyes looking into his. The jaws of the young male crocodile with the damaged tail crunched together with the force of several tonnes. The egg lay undamaged in the hot sun while the crocodile dragged his one-and-a-half-metre prey to the water. At the water's edge, he placed his forefeet on the corpse and held it down while he tore off and swallowed a limb. Some time later, when digestion had taken place, he would regurgitate the indigestible portion and spit it out. In the meantime, he dragged the lizard into the water and swam to a point where the water ran past steep banks. Here, he pushed the lizard into a niche where it jammed fast. When he was hungry again, he would return to eat more of it.

In the afternoon, the big male made his way through the marshy ground to a quiet pool situated about half a kilometre inland. Pa-

These estuarine crocodiles are bred on a special crocodile farm in Singapore. Their skins are used for such luxury items as handbags, shoes, briefcases and belts. However, only the soft hide of the belly is suitable as, unlike the back and tail, it is not covered by bony plates. Indiscriminate hunting of crocodiles is discouraged or even prohibited by many countries as it has endangered many species. However, legalised farming is permitted in Cuba, Japan, Singapore and parts of the United States where crocodiles are bred for this purpose without threatening their numbers in the wild.

tiently and silently he slipped into the pool and cruised into the shadow of an overhanging tree. The rim of the pool was pocked with hoof prints that showed its popularity among thirsty gazelles and zebra. The crocodile was barely visible in the water. Little more than his eyes and the tip of his snout were above the surface. His wait was shorter than usual. A family of warthogs trotted down to the waterhole, to a spot on the opposite side of the pool.

He was about to begin a slow approach to them when a sitatunga, a small gazelle, nervously stepped to the edge of the pool close by him. It stood looking carefully around for some minutes before walking daintily a few steps into the water. It bent its head to drink, alert but not alert enough to see the lurking crocodile inch smoothly through the water towards its lapping tongue. The algae swirled hardly at all as the great reptile's tail gently pushed it through the

In Australia, indiscriminate hunting with high-powered rifles has reduced the numbers of the native estuarine crocodile. They are now protected by government legislation against excessive hunting. The estuarine crocodile, found throughout a long arc stretching from Sri Lanka through Malaysia and northern Australia to the Fiji islands, differs from the Nile crocodile in that it has no post-occipital scutes on its back. Reaching up to 10m in length, it has scute-like bony ridges along its snout. It lives at the mouths of rivers and in saltwater and may be seen swimming between islands many kilometres from the coast.

Fights, such as this one, between rival male crocodiles usually follow a well-established sequence of ritualised actions and movements. Both crocodiles try to grab each other by the jaws but although the battle appears rough, it is rare for one of the reptiles to be seriously hurt or wounded and the conflict ends with the victorious animal banishing the loser from its territorial waters. As they fight the crocodiles roar loudly and thrash about in the water with their great tails. Fights usually come about when a newcomer or a younger member of the group challenges an older crocodile with seniority.

water. It was very near. The powerful tail curved away from the sitatunga like a loaded spring. With a huge foaming swish, the spring was released and the crocodile's tail scythed towards the startled sitatunga, sweeping the animal's feet from under it. The blow carried it out into deep water, and one snap of the crocodile's jaws carried the mammal under water. It would have been hard to say whether it died of drowning or of shock.

The crocodile carried the body further into the deep water. He was hungry. Taking a bite across one of the animal's haunches, the crocodile began to rotate, twisting in the water and churning the surface into a muddy foam. The rotation was so powerful that the haunch tore free of the creature's body. The crocodile carried its prize in its jaws to the surface, where it tossed it about to get it into position to swallow. Carrying the rest of the carcass to the lake took some time and it was dusk before the remains were safely cached away under a bank which overhung the lake.

As the light faded, the group of crocodiles padded down the beach and into the water, heading out into the lake. They made their way steadily towards the mouth of a river up which fish swam to spawn before the rainy season's floods brought the fish fry down again. The water temperature fell three or four degrees below the crocodiles' body temperature. The larger crocodiles simply lay in the water with their mouths wide open to scoop up passing fish. The younger, faster-moving reptiles twisted and turned and snapped up any fish within their range. For many of the crocodiles there was no great urgency in the hunt. They were satisfied with the score or so of water snails they had taken from the water cabbage at the fringe of the lake. They could wait some days before eating a full meal.

As the dusk thickened, the crocodiles continued their confident cruising of the lake. Once they had achieved the critical size of two and a half metres, these great primeval creatures had few enemies, and as night approached they had little to fear from their one formidable enemy – man.

This young crocodile of one or two years old is feeding on cut fish at an Australian crocodile experimental farm. When they are very young, the baby crocodiles feed on worms, beetles, dragonflies, mosquito larvae, crabs and frogs, but as they grow the amount of insects in their diet diminishes and they graduate to snails, fish and eventually waterbirds and even small mammals. They catch their prey by swimming stealthily towards it and pouncing on it with jaws open wide. During the first few weeks of life they remain hidden in the water and even climb onto shrubs to avoid being eaten by older crocodiles.

Species of crocodile

Nile crocodile (*Crocodylus niloticus*) See *At a glance* panel.

The **African long-nosed crocodile** (*Crocodylus cataphractes*) is also called the African gavial because of its long, slender snout. Its head is spotted darkly with brown on a ground of olive-ochre. Dark stripes cross its body and its forehead rises in a dome shape. The African long-nose lives in the belt of forest that stretches across Senegal and the Gambia to north Angola, and east to Lake Tanganyika.

The **African broad-fronted crocodile** (*Osteolaemus tetrapsis*), sometimes called the dwarf crocodile, has prominent brow ridges and a broad snout. The scales on its back and belly are bony and unlike the Nile crocodile, its eyes are a beautiful brown. Its skin is dark brown, and a few specimens have light markings on their backs. It inhabits forest waterholes in Cameroon and Liberia. There are two subspecies of the dwarf crocodile: *O. tetrapsis tetrapsis*, which has an enlarged tip to its nose; and *O. t. osborni*, which lives in the upper Congo river system and has no such enlarged tip.

The **mugger** (*Crocodylus palustris*), or marsh crocodile, is much like the Nile crocodile, but lives in India. It has a short, blunt muzzle and a square of four nuchal shields. Its olive coloured skin darkens with age. Muggers live in a belt from the Sind to Assam, and some have been reportedly seen in Burma. In Sri Lanka lives a subspecies *C. p. kimbula*, with dorsal scales different from those of the mainland species.

The **Siamese crocodile** (*Crocodylus siamensis*) has a narrower muzzle than that of the mugger, and a keel or ridge stretches forwards from between its eyes to its nose. The Siamese crocodile is found in Assam, parts of Indochina and on the island of Java.

The **false gavial** (*Tomistonia schlegelii*) has the narrowest snout of any crocodile and eats little other than fish. Unlike most of the crocodile family, whose jaws fuse about eight teeth from their noses, the false gavial's join at about 14 teeth from the tip of its snout. It lives in Malaya, Sumatra and Borneo.

The **New Guinea freshwater crocodile** (*Crocodylus novaeguineae*) has a rather more pointed muzzle than that of the Siamese crocodile. It can live in mountain habitats up to 1 550m above sea-level. A subspecies, the Philippines crocodile (*C. n. mindorensis*), has a keel on its snout, but this is less well defined than on the New Guinea variety.

The **Australian freshwater crocodile** (*Crocodylus johnstoni*), sometimes called Johnston's crocodile after its discoverer, has a narrow muzzle. Its diet consists mainly of fish. Johnston's crocodile lives in equatorial Australia, north of a line between Derby and Cairns.

The **broad-snouted caiman** (*Caiman latirostris*) has a broader snout than the spectacled caiman's but has a similar 'pair of spectacles'. Its eyelid ridges are sometimes protected by by small horny protuberances. It lives in the swamps and rivers of Paraguay and Brazil.

The **black caiman** (*Melanosuchus niger*) is called the big caiman by Brazilians. It has no arrangement of 'spectacle' ridges. A ridge between the eyes exists but is not prominent as in other caimans, and its snout is rather like an alligator's. Black caimans are now only rarely found in their territories in the Amazon basis and the Guianas.

The **smooth caimans** (*two species: Palaeosuchus palpebrosus* and *P. trigonatus*) live in the Amazon basin. Both have bony skin plates, more ossified (bony) than those of any other crocodilian. The way the scales of their armour interlock is closely related to the arrangement of scales of some prehistoric reptiles.

The large **American alligator** (*Alligator mississipiensis*) has a flattish head and short, rounded snout. A bony septum separates its nostrils, and it has two nuchal shields. Its legs are less strongly developed than those of the African crocodiles. The alligator is clumsier both on land and in the water than the crocodiles, and it is less aggressive. Alligators have a yellow underbelly, darkening in a mature animal to a blackish shade on the back. The majority of American alligators are found in Florida.

The **Chinese alligator** (*Alligator sinensis*) lives in the swamplands of the lower Yangtse River. Its belly is protected with bony plates, and it has strongly developed ridges over the eyes. Its snout is shorter than the American alligator's and its belly is spotted and streaked with yellow and grey, merging into a greenish black.

The **spectacled caiman** (*Caiman crocodilus*) derives its name from the ridged eyelids that are linked across the bridge of its muzzle, making it look as though it is wearing spectacles. Its belly is nearly white and shades to an olive-brown colour on top. The four varieties of this caiman *C. c. crocodylus, C. c. apopoensis, C. c. fucus* and *C. c. yacara*) live in the Amazon and Orinoco basins.

Nile crocodile

American alligator

The **American crocodile** (*Crocodylus acutus*) also swims out to sea and its colour, too, resembles that of the estuarine crocodile but turns a characteristic grey with age. It lives in rivers and on islands between latitudes 5° south and 30° north in the New World.

The **Orinoco crocodile** (*Crocodylus intermedius*) is named after the Orinoco river system where it lives. Its snout is more pointed and slender than that of the American crocodile.

The **Cuban crocodile** (*Crocodylus rhombifer*) is on the verge of extinction, now living only in the Zapata Swamp in Cuba. The two ridges across its forehead nearly meet the lines of its orbits (bow ridges) to form a rough rhomb, from which it derives its Latin name.

Morelet's crocodile (*Crocodylus morleti*) has a swollen area in front of its eyes, rather like a similar feature on the African crocodile. Morelet's crocodile, too, is much reduced in numbers.

The **estuarine crocodile** (*Crocodylus porosus*), sometimes called the saltwater crocodile, is the largest of all the crocodilians. Specimens well over six metres were reported in the past, but this would now be considered exceptional. The snout of the estuarine crocodile is two-and-a-quarter times as long as it is wide at the base. The crocodile's back has six or eight rows of raised plates, but has no nuchal plates.

The gavial (*Gavial gangeticus*) has an extraordinarily long, narrow snout, an adaptation for hunting and catching fish, which is its principal food. Its mouth is equipped with 54-58 teeth in the upper jaw and 50-51 teeth in the lower one.

Gavial

Caiman

Johnston's crocodile

Crocodile appetite

Often accused of having and indulging a huge appetite, the crocodile has, in fact, surprisingly modest food requirements. It eats about 50 full meals each year, with snacks of a light nature in between. Its metabolism (food to energy conversion) runs at a slow rate. The food intake of a captive 2.30m crocodile which weighed 45kg averaged 312g per day. It is unlikely that the appetite of a crocodile in its natural habitat would be substantially greater although its more active life would increase its requirements a little.

The crocodile's stomach is not large, so although the reptile will killl large prey from time to time it will take a long time to eat them, several days in many cases. The stomach has two chambers. The larger one is rather like a gizzard whereas the other, reached through a small, nearly round hole, resembles an appendix and leads to the intestines. Digestion is slow but fairly efficient, and the crocodile excretes solids only about once a week or even less frequently.

As one might expect, a crocodile's eating habits alter as it grows to maturity. The youngest crocodiles eat dragonfly nymphs, water beetles and other insects. As the reptiles grow to about 1.50m, they include frogs, snails and small fish in their diet while rapidly learning to capture larger fish. By the time they have grown to about two metres in length, the crocodiles lose some of the nimbleness needed to capture fish easily so they turn their attention increasingly to mammals and birds. Many of the most popular prey are not large; the stomach contents of a 2.70m crocodile were analysed to show that it had recently eaten 40 rats, whereas a 3.68m crocodile's stomach contained no more than about 90 snails.

Growth

A crocodile's growth over the first seven years of its life averages about 26.5cm in good conditions, but this can be accelerated or stunted by either unusually good or poor conditions in the animal's environment. Pygmy crocodiles occur in parts of Africa where pools are heavily contaminated with minerals leached out of the surrounding soil and where the reptiles have to aestivate for long periods. When crocodiles aestivate their metabolism slows down and they become torpid. They may lie quite still in the chambers of their burrows or they may bury themselves in mud to endure the long dry season, just as a bear, elsewhere, will hibernate to survive the long cold season.

The crocodile's rate of growth slows down until, at the age of about 22 years, it grows an average of only 3.6cm in length each year. As increase in length slows down, growth in bulk steps up and the girth becomes more impressive. A female crocodile lays her first eggs between eight and 12 years of age, whereas males mature sexually at around 10 years old.

About 40 eggs are laid by the female crocodile, each separated from the next by earth and buried under the ground. The surface, usually of sandy or loamy earth, is smoothed over so that there is no sign of the nest itself. While the eggs are incubating in the warm soil, the mother guards them from the shade of an overhanging bush or tree, until the young crocodiles start to squeak in their shells 11 to 14 weeks later. At this point the mother uncovers the eggs and the young break through their eggshells and hatch.

From the egg to the river

The female crocodile chooses the site for her nest with care. Often she will share a nesting site with other females. On one site, only 64m square, a naturalist discovered 24 nests. The crocodile scrapes a hole between 20 and 50cm deep and lays her eggs in several batches, scattering earth between them so that the eggs do not touch and endanger their shells. Finally, she covers them with about 10cm of soil and smooths the surface flat. She chooses a site which is near some shade from which she can watch the hidden nest, staying on guard except when she must swim to find food. Meanwhile, the temperature in the nest remains at 30° to 35°C, with a variation of only about plus or minus 3°C.

At the end of the incubation period (11 to 14 weeks) the young ones start to squeak inside the shells. The mother can hear through the covering of earth to a distance of about 4m. The hatching crocodiles break through their shells by pushing an egg tooth, a sharp piece of lime on the ends of their noses, against the protective wall until it cracks open. There is quite a struggle before the baby can wriggle free of the shell, and sometimes the mother joins in, taking the egg in her mouth and gently cracking it to help the young crocodile into the world.

The hatchlings have a yolk sac attached to them. It is about the size of a hen's egg and provides them with nourishment in addition to the food they capture for themselves. The sac gradually shrinks until it finally disappears after several months. When the hatchlings emerge from their shells, the wet season is filling the rivers and pools, providing the young crocodiles with an ideal environment in which to begin their lives. Few of these creatures will survive the journey to the water and the attacks of predators once they take to their natural element. Storks, fish eagles, monitor lizards and other crocodiles often snap them up before they can defend themselves.

For two or three weeks the young crocodiles stay together, guarded by their mother and by other mature females. Then they form new groups with young crocodiles from other nests, quickly learning to hide themselves away, especially from other crocodiles. It is hard to observe crocodiles between 60cm and 1.15m long in the wild. They conceal themselves, possibly in deep burrows and sometimes trekking miles across country to find safe waterholes. Their danger is so great that only between two and five per cent of the hatchlings survive to reach adulthood.

This picture sequence shows how the young crocodile, a miniature replica of the adult, emerges from the egg, about three months after the eggs are laid by the mother. When the young begin to grunt within the shells, the mother scrapes away the protective covering of earth and the babies gradually break their way through the shells and clamber out of the eggs. At this stage they are about 30cm in length. Their mother leads them down to the nearby water where they remain hidden for the first few weeks of their lives.

Ready to ambush
Largest of all living reptiles, the crocodile is highly adapted to a life spent mostly in the water or near to it. The position of the eyes, nostrils and ears high on the head enable the animal to lie nearly submerged in the water while these senses are all operating effectively. Its eyes, with their vertically slit-shaped pupils, are sited in knobby protrusions which rise proud of the skull. The nostrils open from a swelling at the tip of the upper snout, and the ear flaps lie a little behind the eyes.

The crocodile is a well-equipped ambusher: its eyesight is good, the pupils opening wide at night to absorb the maximum light and giving good night vision when most of the reptile's hunting is done. The upper and lower lids offer effective protection to the eyeballs, and a third lid moves from the inner corner across the eye to protect it under water. This lid is known as the nictating membrane; it is thin and transparent so the crocodile can use this protection in the muddy waters of a lake or slow-moving river and can still look for food. The crocodile's sight is thought to improve with maturity. This improvement may relate to its increased hunting range. When mature, it can pick out moving objects at 33m, and experiments show that its colour perception is quite well developed.

The crocodile's sentinel
For long discounted as a traveller's 'tall tale', it is now accepted that there are birds which have a strangely trusting and mutually profitable relationship with crocodiles. The earliest account of this odd alliance is found in the writings of the Greek traveller and historian Herodotus (c.480-430BC), who observed:

> 'All other birds and beasts avoid him (the crocodile), but he is at peace with the trochilos, because he receives benefit from that bird. For when the crocodile gets out of the water on land, and then opens its jaws which it does most commonly towards the west, the trochilos enters its mouth and swallows the leeches. The crocodile is so well pleased with this service that it never hurts the trochilos.'

The trochilos is now believed to be the spur-winged plover or, perhaps, the Egyptian plover. These birds, and a few others, to a lesser extent, live close to crocodiles. They clean the great reptiles' mouths of fragments of food and parasites, and they also warn the crocodile of the approach of danger. It is for this reason that the Arabs call the Egyptian plover *ter-el-temsack*, which means 'crocodile's sentinel'. The water dikkop, grey wagtail, egret and marabou stork also show this behaviour, but not always with safety. Marabous have been found in the stomachs of dead crocodiles.

Crocodiles are a living meal for many parasites. Leeches infest their mouths, eyelids and nostrils and suck the reptile's blood. The biting fly, *Glossina palpalis*, feeds on the eyelids, neck and joints of the hindlegs. Its habit of infecting the blood with sleeping sickness and other diseases seems to have little effect on the crocodile. The reptile suffers more seriously from the attentions of the nematode worms that live in its stomach. These weaken the animal, in some cases seriously.

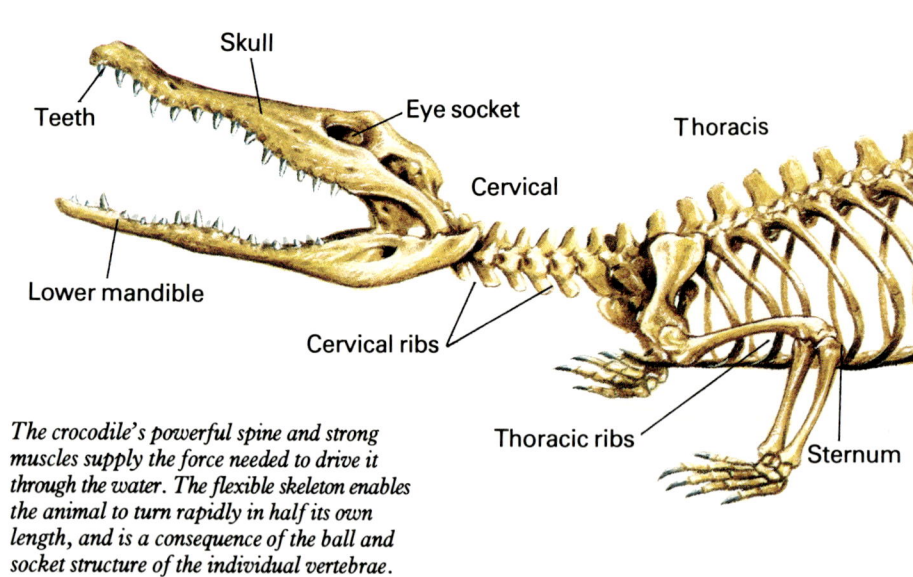

The crocodile's powerful spine and strong muscles supply the force needed to drive it through the water. The flexible skeleton enables the animal to turn rapidly in half its own length, and is a consequence of the ball and socket structure of the individual vertebrae.

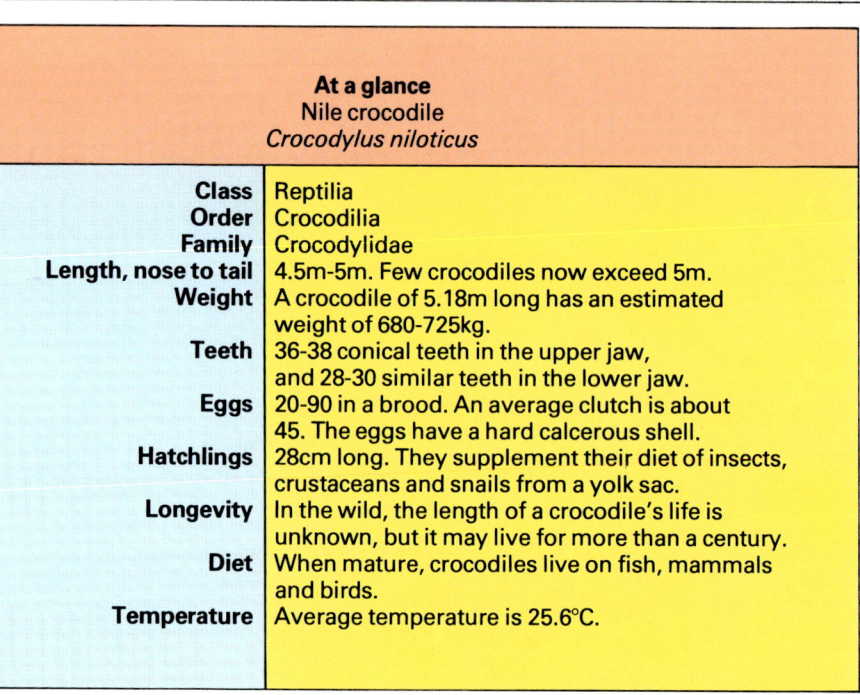

At a glance Nile crocodile *Crocodylus niloticus*	
Class	Reptilia
Order	Crocodilia
Family	Crocodylidae
Length, nose to tail	4.5m-5m. Few crocodiles now exceed 5m.
Weight	A crocodile of 5.18m long has an estimated weight of 680-725kg.
Teeth	36-38 conical teeth in the upper jaw, and 28-30 similar teeth in the lower jaw.
Eggs	20-90 in a brood. An average clutch is about 45. The eggs have a hard calcerous shell.
Hatchlings	28cm long. They supplement their diet of insects, crustaceans and snails from a yolk sac.
Longevity	In the wild, the length of a crocodile's life is unknown, but it may live for more than a century.
Diet	When mature, crocodiles live on fish, mammals and birds.
Temperature	Average temperature is 25.6°C.

Two birds, the spur-winged and Egyptian plovers, live symbiotically with the Nile crocodile, cleaning fragments of food and parasites from the reptile's great mouth and warning the crocodile of the approach of danger without harm to themselves. Both birds are widely distributed in a long belt which stretches right across central Africa, and the spur-winged plover is even found as far north as the shores of the Black Sea in Europe.

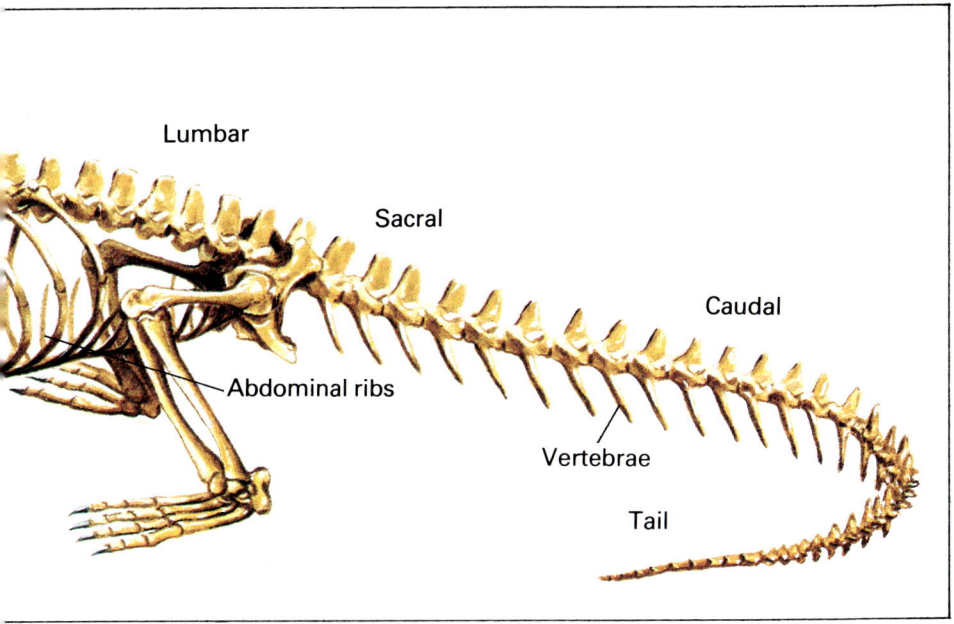

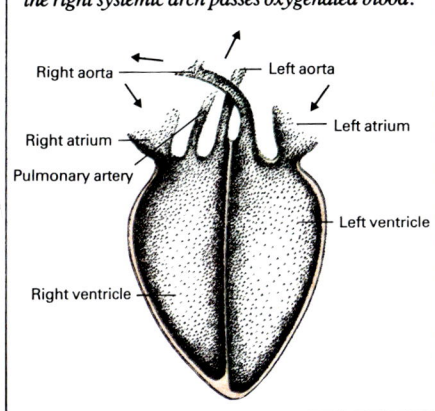

The crocodile's heart is unusual for a reptile, helping to equalise the pressure between the veinous and arterial systems. This enables the crocodile to remain submerged for long periods. The panizzae foramen allows the pulmonary artery to receive de-oxygenated blood while the right systemic arch passes oxygenated blood.

The graceful swimming action of the crocodile makes full use of the flexible tail, which pivots on the rigid forward part of the skeleton. The legs are held close to the sides of the body except when they are used to assist in a turning manoeuvre. The force required to drive the reptile through the water is provided by the muscles and the powerful spine.

The crocodile and alligator are very similar in appearance and only an expert can distinguish between them. In order to tell the difference one must look closely at their snouts and teeth. The alligator has a blunter snout and its upper teeth overlap the lower ones when it shuts its mouth. However, the crocodile's teeth align and engage when it closes its mouth. Both are members of the order Crocodylia but alligators are native only to the USA and China.

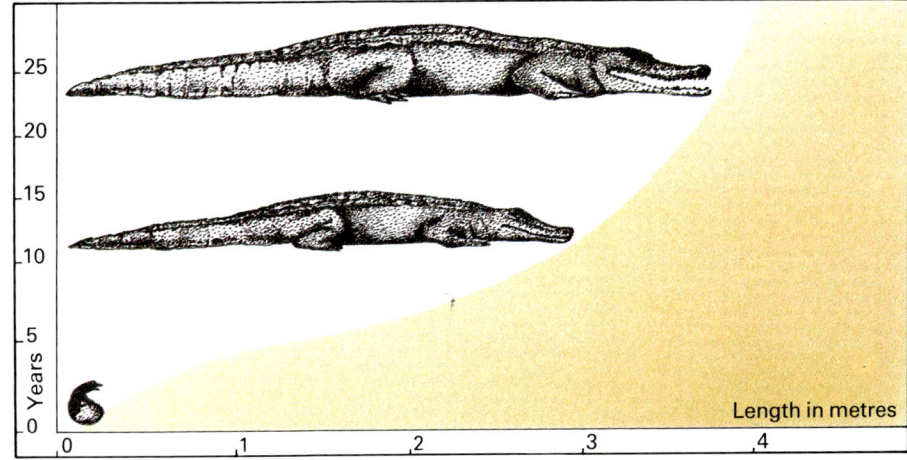

This growth chart shows the rate at which young crocodiles grow throughout their early years, as measured in metres. In the first seven years of life, a crocodile's growth averages about 26.5cm per year in good conditions, but this may be accellerated or even stunted by unusually good or poor conditions. As it grows older, its growth rate slows down until, at the age of about 22 years, it grows an average of only 3.6cm in length each year. However, as increase in length slows down, growth in the reptile's bulk speeds up and the crocodile looks more powerful.

The Salmon

The peat-dark waters ran brown as ale and clear as cairngorm over the large round pebbles of the burn's bed. The flow was brisk, water catching at the heath grasses that overhung the bank and sending bubbles banging by the small boulders that lay scattered in its path. The river here was in its grayling stage, a little less than 20m wide, and with gravel-bottomed shallows at its margins where the water gurgled past the banks. A little below a gentle bend in the river, the bank rose above the tall grasses which hung over a small pool of deep water. Here it was dark and the early morning light gleamed from the surface, making it hard to see the barely moving shapes in its cold interior.

Deep down, the silvery-brown salmon faced upstream, her tail moving slowly from side to side as she held her station in the pool. For nearly two hours she had idled as the morning light filtered down to her, sending mottled patterns across the silty bottom of the pool. She did not seem to be in very good condition. The journey she had made upstream from the river mouth had been long – for four months she had swum against the flow of water, sometimes drifting back, tail-first down the current, but steadily over the weeks she had swum towards the spawning ground. The water scent that filled her nostrils urged her upriver to some place she would recognise.

When she had swum in from the deep sea in early June, drawn to the coast from which her native river emptied into the sea, she had patrolled slowly along the shelf of rock that lifted up from the deeps and contoured the shallow seas that led to the land. The light of the sun moved through the clear air above her and, day by day, she had used this beacon as her guide, compensating for its move-

The salmon leaping a river (opposite) and a small waterfall (below) are swimming upstream from the sea to breed in their natal streams. This migration takes place in late winter or late summer and may be hazardous and arduous as the salmon overcome the many obstacles in their path, determinedly leaping rocks, rapids and waterfalls on their journey to their birthplace. Scientists do not understand fully how the salmon find their way back through the oceans to their natal river, although it has been suggested that they make use of ocean currents, smells, tastes, the salinity and oxygen content of the water or may even be guided by celestial navigation or the Earth's magnetic field. Their journey remains, nevertheless, one of the astonishing feats of nature.

31

These brown bears are fishing for salmon on the North American coast. Bears catch many salmon when they gather at the mouths of rivers before running upstream to their ancestral birthplace to spawn.

ment so that her course remained constant. But as the coast had barred her horizon, she turned to swim parallel to it. She had 'tasted' the waters, seeking the home taste: the smell she remembered from the days when she had swum out from the fresh waters to the salty sea two-and-a-half years earlier. It had been some days before the home smell had flared along her senses and faded again. Then she had found the trail, faint at first but as she followed it grew stronger. The estuary was broad and she had bathed her silver scales in its waters. The orange tints of her sleek body had thrown back the pure light of the northern summer sun as she swam near the surface of the sea-green waves.

The salmon had paused in the waters of the estuary with her companions, a small shoal of 15 others which had won their way to the mouth of the salmon river. Their journey had been hard right from the beginning. Its dangers had nearly overwhelmed them even as the great fish swept in vast silver shoals through the feeding-grounds in the deep cold waters south of Greenland. It was here, when they were hunting herring, that thousands of salmon had darted into a huge mesh which hung like a curtain of weed in the water. The net had gathered them together in a panic-ridden heap and hauled them out of the water into the burning air to dump them on to the hard deck of a ship. Males and females, ripe for the spawning trek, their aquatic skills now useless to help them, died on the ship. The female salmon, however, had been lucky. She had been near the rim of the net and, just before it tightened, an anguished flick of her tail drove her through the air to land in clear water beyond. With a score of others, she swam rapidly from danger. She had been in prime condition and easily stayed with the shoal while it covered more than 80km that day.

For weeks the salmon shoal had threaded its way through the food-rich sea, moving south-west steadily. Other members of the shoal had met disasters on the way. The biggest salmon of all, a fine remade kelt which had been making the journey home for the second time, a fringe of gill maggots clinging to his gill slits, had twisted and darted in frantic evasion of a hunting seal. The chase had continued for several minutes, sometimes passing through the shoal itself, before the seal rolled over and, with a powerful surge of her hind flippers, had bitten deep into his belly. Later, a pair of small dog sharks had taken four more of the shoal before it reached the waters of the estuary.

The salmon had waited in the brackish water for several days. One evening, the flow of river water had grown much stronger as the spate from a summer storm that deluged the inland hills had swept downriver to the sea. That night, the salmon broached the tidal and river currents to swim into the **mainstream** of the river. The 16 survivors had been in prime condition – none weighed less than 10kg – although they had fed hardly at all since their arrival in the estuary. Occasionally they had snapped at small fish or, as they had swum into the river, at an insect on the surface. The fishes' appetite seemed to have faded away completely. The fat-rich muscle tissue they had built up over the years at sea kept them fit and active but still they snapped instinctively when they saw an attractive fly land in reach on the silvery roof above their heads. It was this reflex that reduced the shoal to 15 fish.

An angler had snaked his line perfectly across the wide waters on the morning of the third day of their upstream migration. His beautifully tied fly had dropped daintily onto the water. A large

33

These salmon are spawning in a small stream near Valdez, Alaska. Spawning usually takes place between September and January, especially in the months of November and December. The males usually dig a redd (spawning ground) in which the female lays about 1600 eggs per kilogramme weight of fish. The male attends her, fertilising the eggs by shedding his milt over them. In order to protect the eggs from predators, the female covers them over with several centimetres deep of gravel and then moves upstream to repeat the process. Depending on the temperature of the water, the eggs hatch five to 21 weeks after the actual spawning.

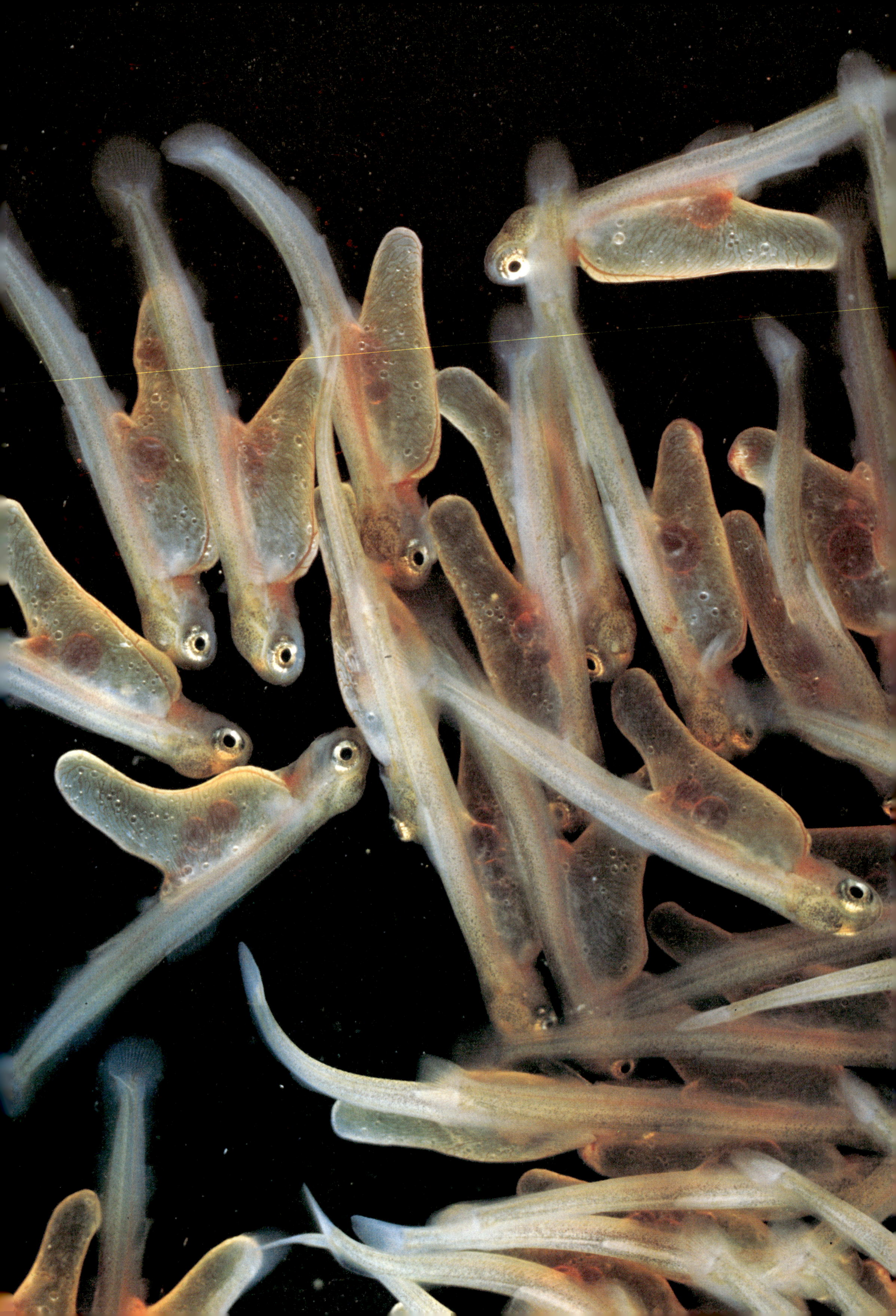

female had casually snapped at it. The hook had struck deep into her upper jaw. For nearly three-quarters of an hour the struggle had continued as she fought to free herself but the angler had drawn her close, gaffed her and thrown her onto the bank with a ringing laugh. A sharp blow had dispatched her life, and the thousands of eggs that lay developing in her perfect body would never know life.

The fresh water of the river had been warmer than the depths of the sea. Unconsciously, the salmon's body had adapted back to the fresh water into which she had been born and in which she had lived for three years before she had swum downriver and out to sea. On this return journey, she had absorbed more water into her blood, thinning it by 12 parts in 100: a change that helped her retain essential salts and was a slight compensation for the loss of weight as her fast continued. The orange-red tinge to her silver body had slowly faded as her weight fell and, as the weeks had passed, she had begun to darken to a browner colour. Her shape had begun to change too. The eggs in her body had grown larger, and her belly had swollen to accommodate them. Among her companions, the males, too, had lost weight. Their skins no longer had the rosy burnished look that they had brought with them from the feasting at sea. The migration up the river had begun to extract its price and their skins were marked by abrasions on which patches of pale fungus grew. Their jaws, too, had changed. The males' lower jaws had begun to curve upwards and their teeth had grown longer. Halfway through the trek, one male could hardly close his mouth, his jaws had developed so ferocious an appearance.

Their progress had not always been a simple matter of swimming upstream against the current. The first serious obstacle was a barrier that stretched across the entire river. This dam controlled the flow of water, making the river impassable to the salmon. Soon, they sensed a strong flow of water to their right. Running parallel to the river was a series of troughs made of concrete. Each was placed a little higher than its neighbour as they climbed upstream towards the top of the dam. A strong flow of water ran down 'V' shaped gaps in the upstream and downstream walls of the troughs. The salmon had dropped down deep in the water at the foot of the first 'rung' in this 'fish ladder' and then, with a tremendous surge of acceleration towards the surface, they had forced their way through the fall of water that poured through the 'V'. One after another, the salmon had swum upwards through the falls of water and up the ladder of troughs that would lead them over the top of the dam and onwards to the headwaters of the river beyond.

A few score kilometres above the dam the flow of water had gradually slackened. A dry spell had brought the river level down and in the warmer, slower currents the salmon made less rapid progress. The weakening of the flow of water came at a point where the salmon had met a fall of water. The river narrowed here and it tumbled down overlapping slabs of rock to the deep pools below. In these pools the salmon had paused. A salmon occasionally swam down deep until it brushed lightly against the floor of small pebbles and sprinted upwards through the thin fall of water, leaping out of the skin of water high into the air in an effort to reach the next pool, which lay at the top of the lowest slide of water. Each attempt had failed. The fish, determined as they were, had twisted over in the air before they reached their target, their tails flailing without finding the resistance of water that would have forced them upwards, and therefore they had fallen back down the slope of rock to the pools

These salmon alevins still have their yolk sacs attached four days after hatching out of the eggs. At this stage they are 1cm only in length. For the first four to eight weeks they remain hidden among the pebbles on the floor of the redd. When the yolk sac is absorbed, the young salmon stay in the redd until they measure 2-5cm in length and then they leave to live in shallow fresh water, where they stay until they begin the long journey down to the sea before returning to breed.

These salmon are in the process of hatching from eggs in a redd. The actual hatching time depends on the temperature of the water. Only about 50 per cent of the eggs laid are fertilised by the male, and only half of these hatch. Many of the eggs are eaten by predatory fish, and even the young fish are at risk from hungry trout and perch and have to hide in the pebbles and amongst the water weeds. They spend the next three to eight years living in fresh water, feeding and growing, before swimming down to the oceans where they live for a further one to six years before returning to their natal stream to breed.

below. Many in the shoal had suffered severe abrasions in the attempts and were in poor condition: thin, with their skins and fins tattered by the bruising upstream migration.

In October, the weather had broken and the dry unseasonal spell had ended. The downpour in the hills brought the river level above normal and a torrent of floodwater had poured over the waterfall with a continuous roar. The change happened within a day and the salmon took immediate advantage of it. Only two of the shoal needed more rest after their great efforts in the drought but the rest began their climb up the waterfall. Each had dived deep and, lashing their bodies and tails from side to side, they had forced themselves up the cascading water, pausing to gather their strength in the still pools of spume-covered water below each of the smooth slabs of schist.

It had been November before the female had found the pool where she now rested. A little above it, on the outer curve of the river, the gravel of the riverbed was perfect for her need. She had swum above it a day earlier, sinking down to touch it gently with her anal fin. Of the pebbles in the spot she favoured, most were between 25 and 50mm across, oval and smooth. Here and there was a much larger one, usually more angular.

A large male butted her gently in the flank and, as she swam away from him, another swam into the pool from below the overhang of the bank. They turned to confront one another with an appearance of great savagery. The interloper's gaping jaws snapped at the crease left by the first male's twisting body as he turned to tear at his opponent's flared gill slits. The tussle did not last more than half a minute. The invader of the quiet pool darted away into the middle of the stream. The successful salmon took a slow turn around the pool and glided to the side of the female.

For half an hour the pair stayed almost still, pointing upstream, but the peace was broken when the male again butted her briskly in the side. The female salmon swam from the pool and appeared to examine the gravel that had caught her interest the previous day. The male darted forward and his body quivered rapidly as he watched her. She sank down until her rounded belly nearly touched the riverbed, then rolled over on one side. She whipped her body from side to side, making an up and down flapping movement which shook the silt and gravel from its place. The silt and smallest stones were carried nearly a metre downstream by the current but the larger pebbles settled again to form a low ridge half a metre from her tail. These lashing motions were so strong that her body was arched in a U-bend, and the stones and silt showered away from her in a cloud. Her mouth gaped open and as her tail swept upwards the gravel was sucked up from its place. As her tail surged down again the current it created forced the debris downstream. After many of these slashing movements, she turned onto an even keel and seemed to feel the bottom of the trench she had cut. Her caudal, pelvic and anal fins delicately tested the newly shaped floor of her redd.

Further upstream, another female had been cutting a redd of her own but, dissatisfied with the site, she drifted backwards down the current until she was level with the more successful female. She edged her way towards the deepening trench and its resting tenant but the contemplated invasion quickly turned to rout as the resident in the trench charged which forced the other female to flee.

The female returned from her excursion and continued to cut her redd deeper, resting for a while now and then. It was several hours later, after great labour, that she lay wearily at the bottom of the completed redd. Her tail lightly touched the narrow gap between two small boulders that rose a few centimetres from the floor. The male had been watching with growing interest as the work neared completion and had fiercely chased away a couple of male salmon parr which had also been hanging around the site. They easily evaded

The salmon fry leave the redd for some shallow and secluded waters where they start to feed on tiny insect larvae. They grow to a length of 10cm in their first year and 15cm in their second, when their oval, blotchy markings turn to a silver pigment and the salmon are termed 'smolts'.

the big fish, looking like mere minnows beside his great bulk; but the parr, too, were male salmon with strong mating instincts, even though they had not yet grown to smolthood ready for the journey to the sea. They did not swim far away but stuck close to the gravel shallows a little downstream of the redd.

The resting female slowly sank downwards until her anal fin touched the floor of the redd. As it brushed the gap between the two boulders, she rose back to her previous position. She continued this bobbing motion for a while before making fine adjustments to the gravel at the foot of the ridge she had piled up.

After half an hour of this fussing with the arrangement of the gravel, the female salmon sank down and gently squirmed into what seemed to be a comfortable position with her belly pressed against the stream but with the front part of her body raised. The watching male seemed to shiver with anticipation as he recognised the signs that showed him the female was ready to lay her eggs.

He saw her mouth gape and quickly swam to her, positioning himself by her side and a little higher in the water than she was. His gill slits were extended wide and he quivered with the excitement of the mating. His milt flowed into the water like a pale cloud as she ejected a stream of transparent eggs between the pair of small boulders at the bottom of the redd. The milt and the eggs mixed together and the eggs were fertilised.

On the bank-side of the female, opposite to the side where the large male quivered, a salmon parr ejaculated his milt at the same time and it mixed with a few of the eggs in the trench. He swam clear before the mating salmon appeared to notice him. The female did not seem to object to her miniature suitor.

As soon as the laying had finished, the female swam a few centi-

When the adult salmon return upstream to spawn they are called grilse. They leave the sea, fat and healthy in good condition with firm, red flesh and a silvery body. They build up a special store of fat in preparation for the hazardous, upstream ascent, but as they fast and encounter many obstacles on the way, they become increasingly weak and their once fine flesh appears pale and watery. Their skin is thick and spongy and black spots materialise on their body. The snouts of males become larger and the lower jaw grows into a grotesque, hooked snarl.

metres upstream and began to cut at the redd again. The strokes of her body lifted the gravel and silt so that they drifted over the eggs, covering them from view. The male swam further upstream in search of another female, while his mate of a few minutes earlier waited for another male to approach and fertilise her next batch of eggs. These would be laid in the same redd and duly covered from sight.

A little way below her redd a couple of the eggs she had just laid drifted away in the current. They had escaped the protection of her trench. A silver flash in the brown water and one of the parr had snapped them up, turning the waste into a nutritious meal.

As the bright ceiling of water above her head faded into a dull bronze in the evening light, the female watched a good-sized male, rather tattered after the journey upstream. He swam round her pool a few times before gliding to her side. Soon she would lay another batch of eggs, about 700 of them, and they would be fertilised by another male. Her great trek upriver had brought her to this climax of her life and over the following eight or nine days she would complete her task of laying around 12,000 to 15,000 eggs. Exhausted, she would drift downstream towards the sea. If she succeeded in descending the waterfalls and the fish ladder she might reach the strengthening, food-rich salt waters again. The males that had fertilised her eggs, too, might make the return journey but few would have the strength to drift more than a few kilometres downstream before they beached their ravaged bodies in the river shallows where the birds would eat their remains.

Down in the safety of the river gravels, the eggs would slowly mature, rich with the hope of another homecoming for the king of fish in the years to come.

After spawning, the exhausted salmon drift downstream in a weakened and emaciated condition. The spent salmon are called kelts and they drop down the river, tail first, back to the sea. Few of them ever reach their destination and die on the way from fasting and disease. However, the fortunate kelts that reach the sea soon start to feed and recover and may return upstream to spawn a second and even a third time despite the dangers and hazards they will have to face.

Common Atlantic (European)

Coho

Chinook

The king of fish
Few people can watch the migration of this large fish, as it presses upstream past waterfalls, rapids and weirs, without investing the salmon with the human virtue of nobility. The cold northern waters were once alive with leaping salmon, which provided a rich source of nourishment for rich and poor alike north of the 40th parallel. Our ancestors, as far back as Magna Carta (1215), legislated against the construction of barriers across rivers in case these might interfere with the salmon's seasonal trek upstream to the spawning shallows. Their care ensured a supply of the fish until late in the nineteenth century when Man's folly turned some of Europe's greatest salmon rivers into sewers of poison which destroyed the great fish. The Thames, Rhine, Douro, Seine and many others died as rivers, becoming mere gutters to run off water fouled by rubbish from towns.

In North America, the picture became as bad as that in Europe. River after river, once rich in salmon, became barred to their migrations. The great fish died in thousands every season as they exhausted themselves in desperate attempts to surmount barriers thrown across their time-honoured routes.

Men were slow to realise the value of what they were losing, but eventually the lesson was learned in some areas and work began on finding new ways of reducing contamination of the rivers and of building structures that bypassed the dams so that the salmon might reach their spawning grounds. However, these problems were tackled late, and the salmon's needs in the design of fish ladders and fish passes over dams are still imperfectly understood. The world remains poor in stocks of Atlantic salmon, despite the massive restocking of rivers from expensive fish hatcheries.

Most fish thrive in either a freshwater or a saltwater environment, but few manage to change from the one to the other as well as the salmon does. It may be that the salmon's ancestors adapted to changes in salinity in the great Ice Age — in the Pleistocene epoch, about two million years ago — when the meltwaters from immense ice sheets poured rivers of fresh water into the northern seas, drastically diluting their salts. About this time, some marine biologists believe, the salmon may have found that spawning in the shallows of rivers offered better chances for their eggs than spawning elsewhere. But no matter how it happened, the low salinity of the seas of the time must have made the transition to a freshwater environment fairly easy; and by the time the seas' saltiness slowly increased, the pattern of the salmon's life was established.

The subfamily *Salmoninae* has five genera — *Brachymystax*, *Salvelinus* (charrs), *Hucho*, *Salmo* and *Oncorhynchus* — of which *Salmo* and *Oncorhynchus* include the fishes that most people would recognise as salmon. The genus *Oncorhynchus* includes five species of Pacific salmon — *O. masou*, *O. kisutch*, *O. keta*, *O. tschawytscha*, *O. nerka* and *O. gorbuscha* — of which all but the first have spawning territories in North America and are described often as North American species, although some spawn in other continents as well. The exception, *O. masou*, spawns in Japanese waters.

The genus *Salmo* includes only one species of true salmon, the Atlantic salmon (*S. salar*, meaning the leaper), and several species of trout.

Atlantic salmon (*Salmo salar*) See *At a glance* panel.

The **chum salmon** (*O. keta*), or dog salmon, is a variety that Soviet fisheries have introduced in the White Sea and the Baltic Sea. The summer forms of the species spawn in the streams that furrow the coastline of the Okhotsk Sea and of the west Kamchatka peninsula. They feed in the Okhotsk Sea. The fall salmon of the species choose the River Amur as their home, and feed as far afield as the coastal waters of Japan and the rich feeding grounds of the Berring Sea.

The **chinook salmon** (*O. tschawytscha*) is also called the spring, king, Quinnant, Sacramento, Tyee and Columbia River salmon. The chinook ranges from the waters of northern China across to Alaska. It breeds as far south as the River Ventura in southern California. This 25-45kg fish matures between 4 and 7 years and probably swims further than any other species of salmon when migrating

At a glance Atlantic salmon *Salmo salar*	
Class	Osteichthyes
Order	Salmoniformes
Suborder	Salmonoidae
Family	Salmonidae
Subfamily	Salmoninae
Genus	Salmo
Length	Male: up to 150cm
	Female: up to 100cm
Weight	Male: up to 36kg
	Female up to 20kg
Eggs	10,000-30,000 laid in a spawning
	Each egg is 5-7mm in diameter.
Incubation	70-200 days required, depending on water temperature.
Swimming speed	Up to 16km/h in short bursts.
Leap	About 3m high and about 5m long.
Lifespan	10 years is probably the maximum.
Distribution	From Kara in the north-eastern Soviet Union to Spain where the population, once large is now slight, and from Iceland across the southern tip of Greenland to Newfoundland and Cape Cod in the USA.
Diet	Crustaceans, sprats, sand eels and herring at sea; daphnia, larvae and freshwater shrimps in rivers.

Chum

Humpback

Sockeye

Some common species of salmon are shown above, including the only species of Atlantic salmon and the five species of Pacific salmon: the chinook, or king; the humpback, or pink; the coho, or silver; the sockeye, or blueback; and the chum, or dog. Because of its fine flavour, firm, red flesh and large size, the chinook is generally considered to be the superior species for eating. The North Pacific salmon species are all confined to the western coast of Canada and the United States. Like the Atlantic salmon, they ascend the rivers and streams on the coast of North America to spawn inland in fresh water.

4,000km up the Yukon river system. In the River Columbia, the building of dams destroyed the chinook's chances of reaching its spawning grounds, but more than a score of breeding stations produce around three-quarters of a million fry each year and release them when they reach fingerling size, at 100 days old.

The **silver salmon** (*O. kisutch*), also called the coho salmon, inhabits Pacific waters from Japan to Alaska, and southwards to California. The silver salmon had spawning streams in the upper reaches of the River Columbia and, like the chinook, it suffered from the building of dams. Fish hatcheries release a quarter of a million fingerlings, at about 14 months of age, annually into the river to help maintain and build up stocks.

The **sockeye salmon** (*O. nerka*) is also known as the red or the blueback salmon. It ranges from Alaska to Japan, and as far south as the River Klamath, California. Its popularity as a food fish has led to its introduction into Maine and other states in the USA.

The **pink salmon** *O. gorbuscha*), or humpback salmon, inhabits waters from Japan to Alaska, and south to California. Over a period of 35-45 days, as the pink salmon migrates upstream dramatic changes occur. The males' teeth grow longer until some fish cannot close thier mouths. The salmon becomes a bright red, and the males also develop large humps on their backs. Their survival rate after spawning is lower than that for any other species of salmon.

Oncorhynchus masou spawns in the rivers of Hokkaido and migrates across Pacific waters where it feeds in the seas between Kamchatka, Japan and Korea.

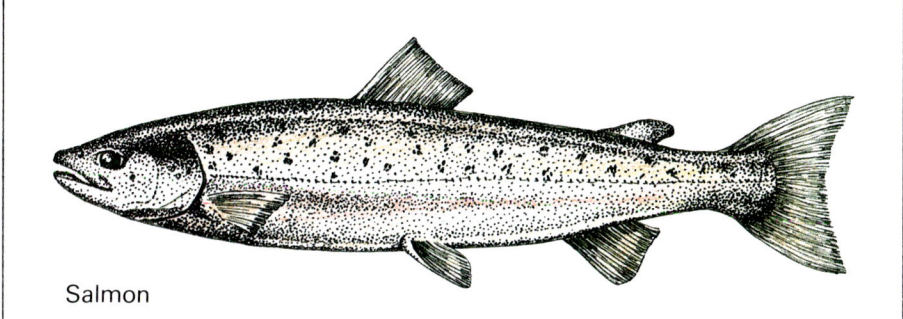

Salmon

Trout

Both salmon and trout belong to the same family, the Salmonidae, and are hatched in fresh water. However, whereas salmon migrate to the sea for a few years before returning to their natal stream to spawn, most trout live entirely in fresh water. A young trout and a young salmon of 12 to 15cm in length are shown above. The salmon's tail is more deeply forked and has a thinner wrist at the end of its body than the trout.

45

Parasites

Salmon are hosts to several parasites in fresh water. At sea, they provide nourishment to the sea louse called *Lepeophtheirus salmonis*. There are more freshwater parasites that live on the salmon, including the carp louse (*Argulus foliaceus*), several species of leech, and a Trematode worm (*Gyrodactylus*). The commonest of the parasites is the salmon gill-maggot (*Salmincola salmonea*).

Once an adult gill-maggot has attached itself to the salmon's gills in fresh water, and matured, it will survive there even when the fish swims out to sea. The parasite's larvae will survive only in freshwater.

The larva of the gill-maggot moves about the salmon's gill filaments until it finds a suitable spot to attach itself before moulting into a second larval stage. Most then moult again to become first-stage females; the males are relatively very few. Male and females then mate, after which the male dies. Six months later, the female lays a batch of eggs. She may lay two more batches before the salmon goes to sea, but if she has no time to lay these batches before the salmon takes to salt water, she waits for the fish to return to fresh water before laying and dying.

The gill-maggot sucks blood from the salmon's gills, but the amount the fish loses is miniscule. The slight injury the salmon suffers is made more serious by the attacks of bacteria in the small ragged scars when the gill-maggots fall from their host. These areas of damaged tissue may be quite large in a salmon that has a large infestation of around 100 gill-maggots.

A supple lever

A salmon, like most other fish, seems to dart from a threat at great speed, but even when making a spurt away from danger, it is unlikely to exceed 16km/h, and fast swimming for a more protracted period would be no faster than about 13km/h. The salmon's top speed depends to a great extent on its size. The larger the fish and the more rapid the beating of its tail from side to side, the faster it will swim. The rule seems to be true when applied to the salmon, but can prove unreliable when the performances of various species of fish are compared.

Fish are built to achieve an excellent accelleration, so that they can sprint after a prey or make a spurt for safety, but they will rarely maintain these high speeds for long. The energy required for these sudden thrusts through the water is extremely great. A fish may apply a thrust of about four times its body weight against the resistance of the water. To achieve this degree of 'lift-off', the fish curves its back acutely to produce an extra wide sweep of its tail, and its muscles will exert about 0.06 horsepower per kilogramme of muscle-weight. The fish will follow up the wide sweep of its tail by rapid movements of the tail. A 280mm fish may swing its tail from side to side 16 times per second, but a larger fish would make fewer movements.

The movement of the fish's tail drives the salmon through the water. This sideways motion of the fish's body has a tendency to twist it sideways, but the water resistance on the sides of the salmon opposes the deviation from the forwards direction.

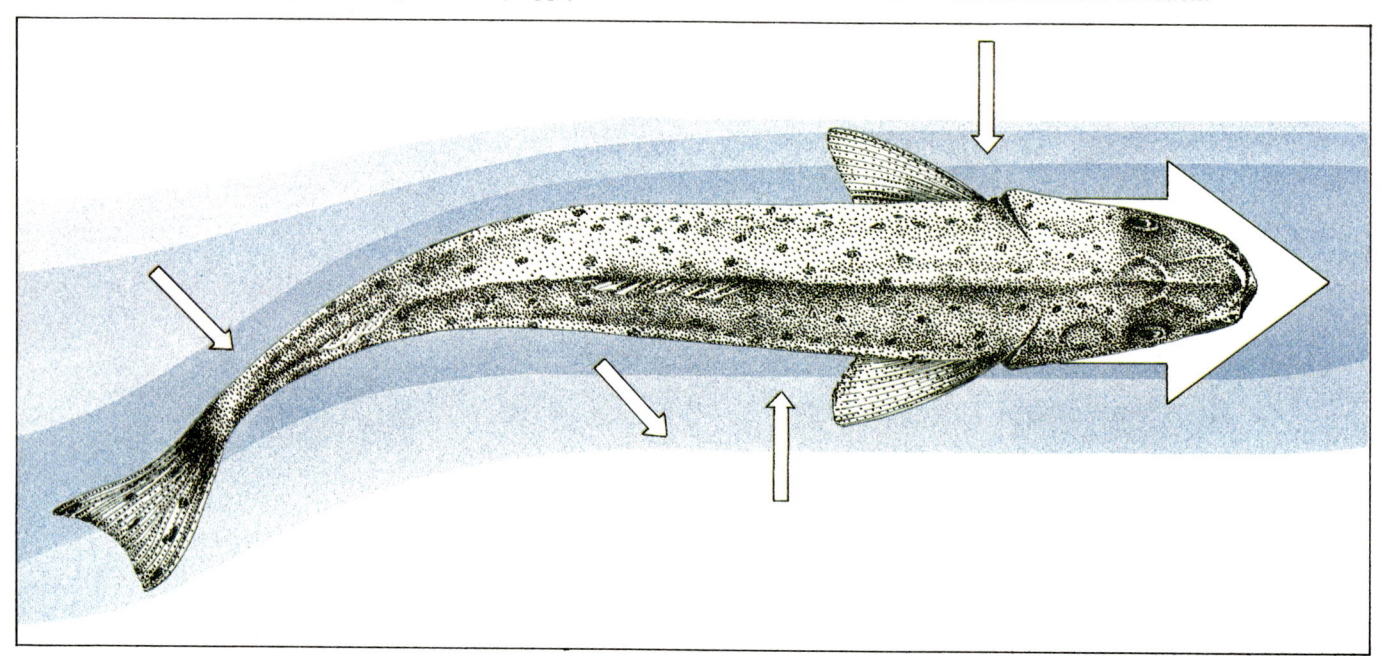

The salmon is driven through the water by the movement of its tail. Although the sideways movement of its body tends to twist it to the side, the water resistance on the salmon's sides opposes the deviation from the forwards direction. The arrows indicate the way in which the water exerts a force on the fish.

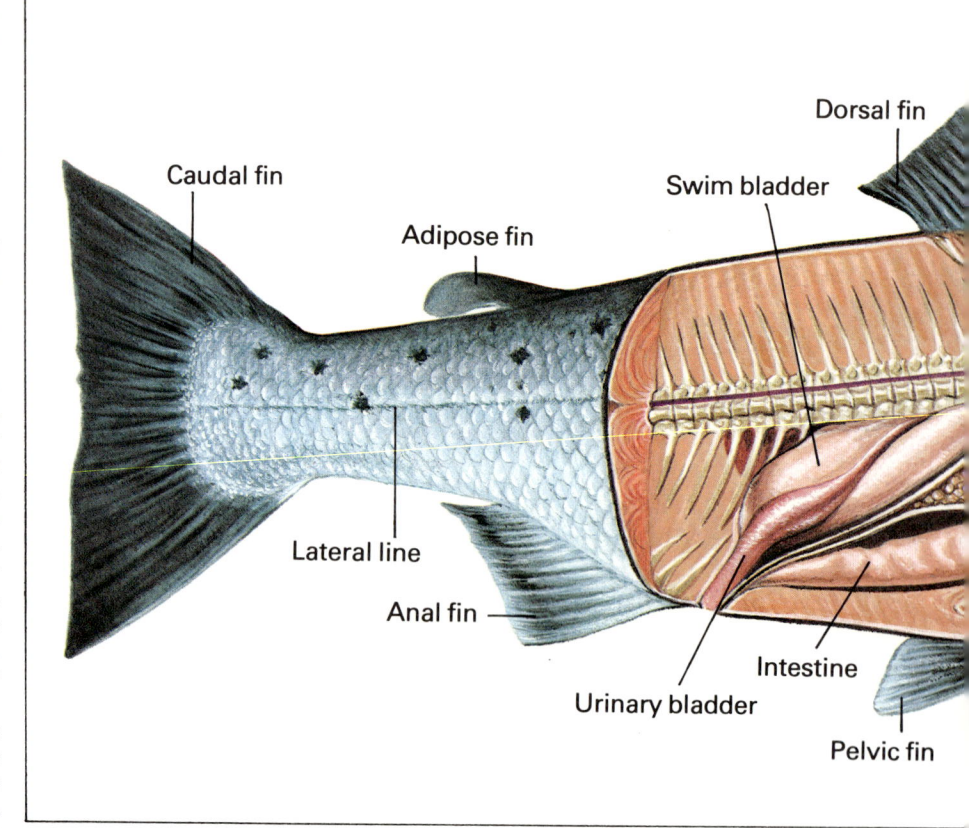

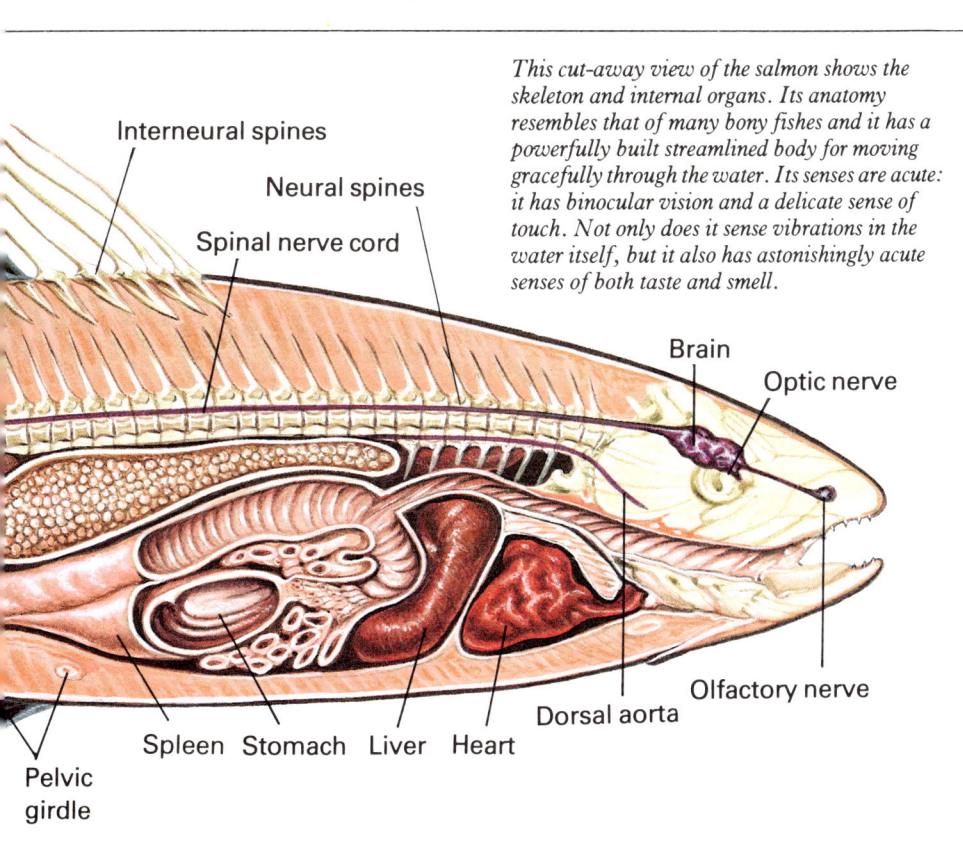

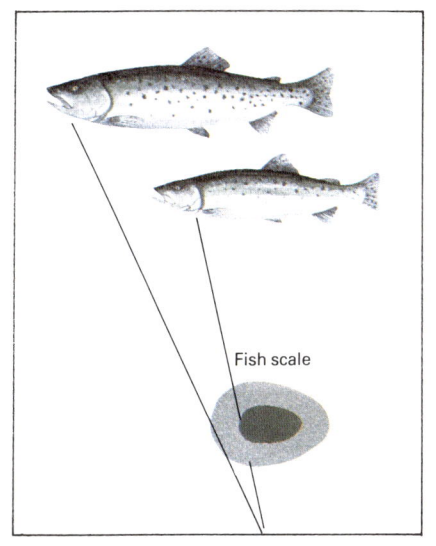

This cut-away view of the salmon shows the skeleton and internal organs. Its anatomy resembles that of many bony fishes and it has a powerfully built streamlined body for moving gracefully through the water. Its senses are acute: it has binocular vision and a delicate sense of touch. Not only does it sense vibrations in the water itself, but it also has astonishingly acute senses of both taste and smell.

- Interneural spines
- Neural spines
- Spinal nerve cord
- Brain
- Optic nerve
- Olfactory nerve
- Dorsal aorta
- Heart
- Liver
- Stomach
- Spleen
- Pelvic girdle
- Fish scale

The salmon's scales start to develop when it is about two or three centimetres long. They grow throughout its life and as they become larger ridges form in their surface, marking the history of their development. These ridges can be used to determine the salmon's age, rather like the growth rings on a tree. The scales do not lie flat against the body but grow obliquely and parallel to one another under a layer of skin. The skin tissue continues inwards.

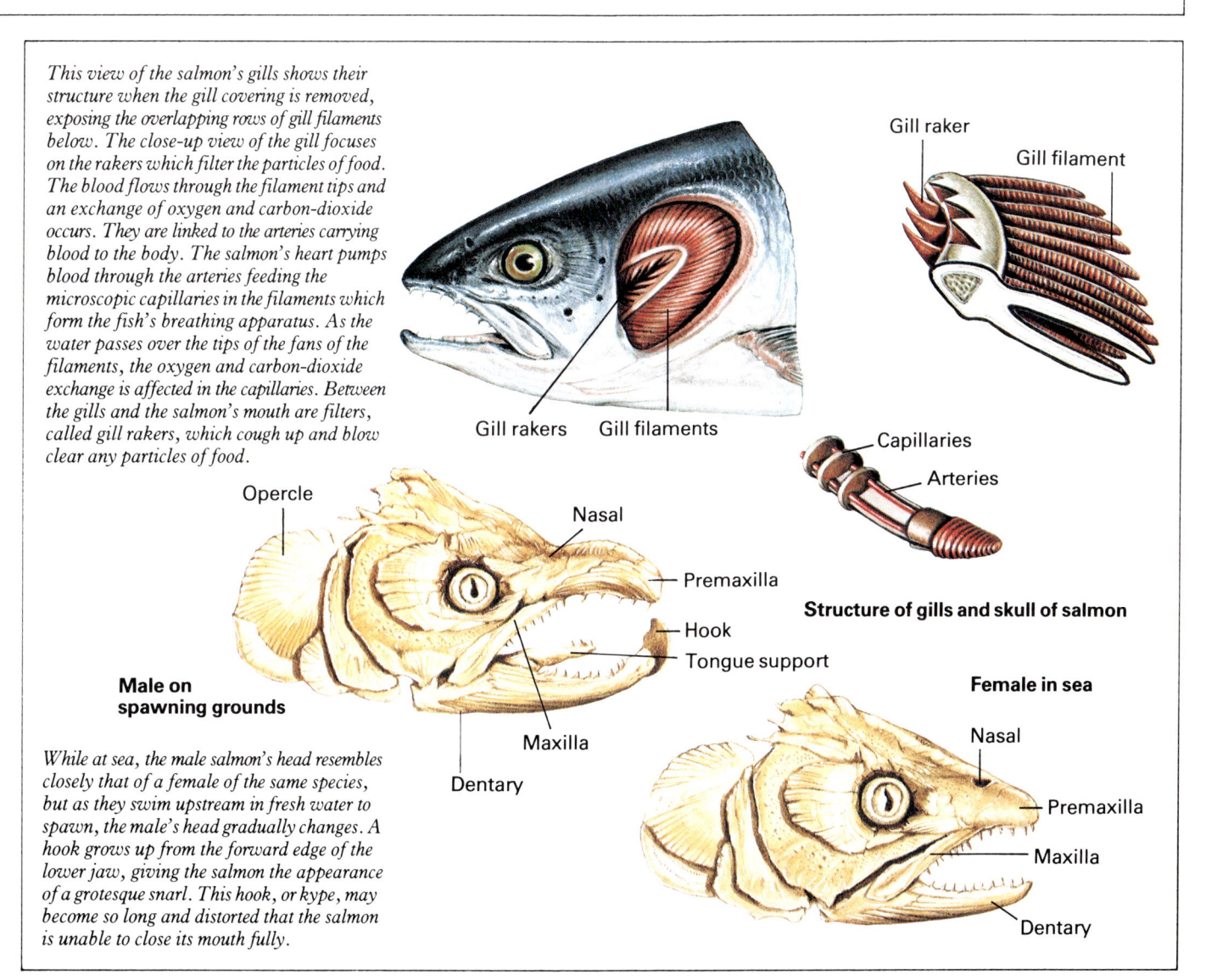

This view of the salmon's gills shows their structure when the gill covering is removed, exposing the overlapping rows of gill filaments below. The close-up view of the gill focuses on the rakers which filter the particles of food. The blood flows through the filament tips and an exchange of oxygen and carbon-dioxide occurs. They are linked to the arteries carrying blood to the body. The salmon's heart pumps blood through the arteries feeding the microscopic capillaries in the filaments which form the fish's breathing apparatus. As the water passes over the tips of the fans of the filaments, the oxygen and carbon-dioxide exchange is affected in the capillaries. Between the gills and the salmon's mouth are filters, called gill rakers, which cough up and blow clear any particles of food.

- Gill raker
- Gill filament
- Gill rakers
- Gill filaments
- Capillaries
- Arteries

Structure of gills and skull of salmon

- Opercle
- Nasal
- Premaxilla
- Hook
- Tongue support
- Maxilla
- Dentary

Male on spawning grounds

Female in sea
- Nasal
- Premaxilla
- Maxilla
- Dentary

While at sea, the male salmon's head resembles closely that of a female of the same species, but as they swim upstream in fresh water to spawn, the male's head gradually changes. A hook grows up from the forward edge of the lower jaw, giving the salmon the appearance of a grotesque snarl. This hook, or kype, may become so long and distorted that the salmon is unable to close its mouth fully.

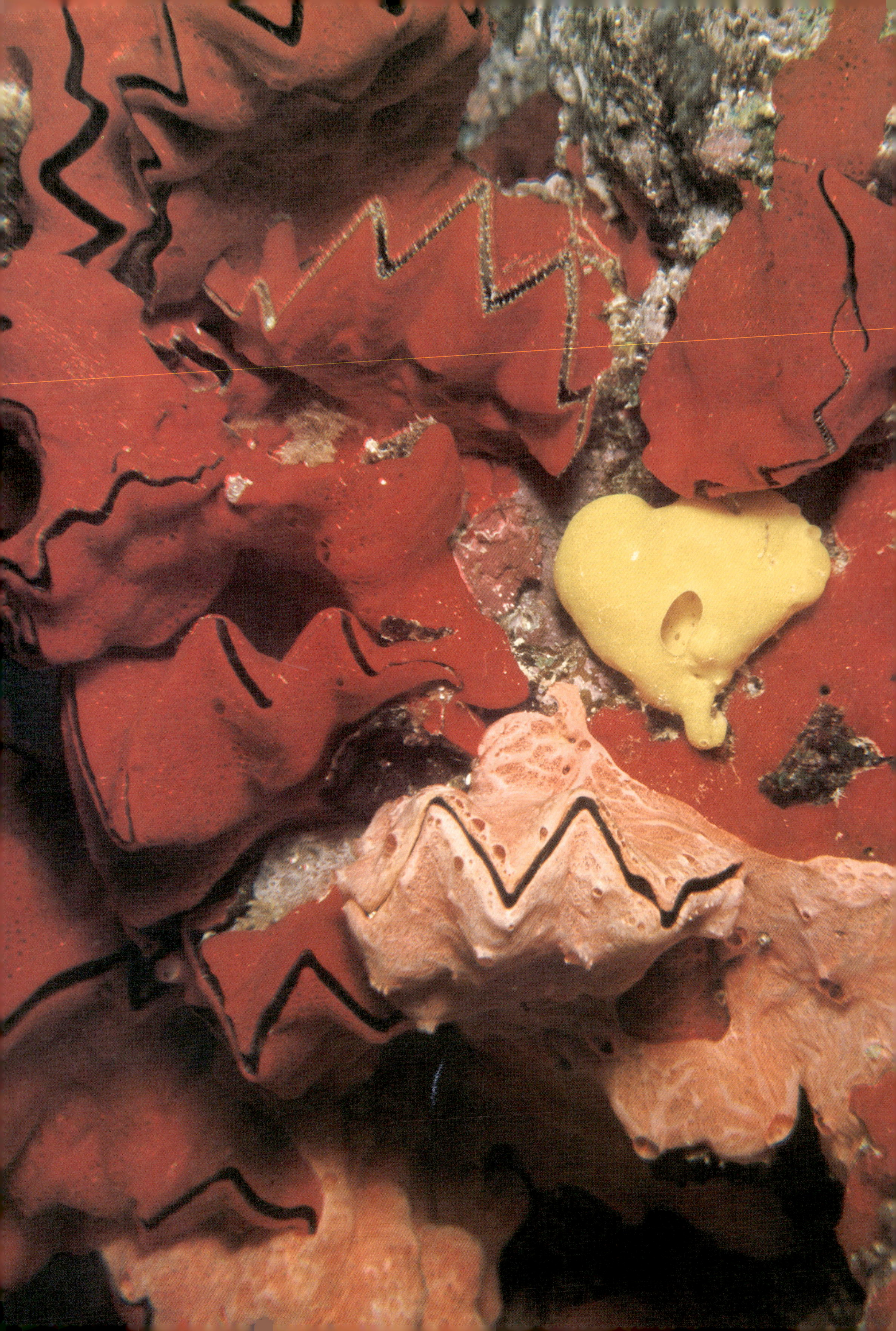

The Oyster

Shells were tight shut against the searing air while the grey oysters lay exposed to the early morning light. The tide had swept out unusually low the night before, leaving the reef of shells and their tangle of eel grass high and dry. The large adductor muscles had clenched the valves shut holding like a rachet mechanism hour after hour. Not until the sun warmed the oysters' flattish upper valves did the ripples of the incoming tide lap over the rough shells.

There was no movement among the oysters even when the sea finally covered them. Round them, in the still shallow water, the soft silt of the tidal harbour swirled densely. When the movement of the unusual tide settled down and the water became clearer, the valves of an oyster on the outer edge of the cluster of shellfish flickered open and puffed out pieces of debris from its feeding the night before. The material floated clear on the current formed by the smartly closing valves and the oyster waited, valves closed.

It was a young oyster, about 60mm from its umbo (beak where the hinge lay) to the opposite margin of the shell. The flat upper valve was marked with a coarse ripple pattern which ran outwards from a centre point about the umbo. The shellfish's shallow-cupped lower valve had a faintly green-grey tinge and its surface was even rougher than the upper shell's.

Nearby, there was a gap in the colony of oysters where a strange cluster of shells clung to the boulder. The shells mounted on one another's backs, twisting slightly to the right. These were newcomers to the harbour, not seen on this coast before; but 300km away to the east, others of their species were successfully competing with oysters for places to attach themselves. More and more oyster larvae, when the time came for them to spatfall (attach themselves to a secure spot for life), found the rocks and harbour piles filled. They were left to drift until overwhelmed by silt or eaten by predators, never having the security to develop their shells fully as a protection against their enemies. The colony of shells piling up on itself was of slipper limpets and they were multiplying rapidly.

The younger oyster's valves parted as its powerful adductor muscle relaxed. The delicate cilia of its middle mantle fold waved rhythmically, creating currents in the surrounding water and drawing in the minute particles of plant life. The shell closed as the adductor contracted. The cilia stroked the food along the gills and then towards the area of the hinge. Behind the hinge, the palps directed acceptable particles towards the oesophagus and the process of final selection and digestion began.

The oyster's valves flicked open to disgorge the particles of food and debris rejected by the palps. As the valves snapped together, the unwanted material jetted well clear. Occasionally, the valves opened to discharge waste products of the digestive process itself. These left the shell on the side opposite to the one through which the oyster inhaled the food-laden water.

The small colony of oysters was swept by a gentle, steady current and the water was clear. The neighbouring mat of eel grass waved sinuously, its movements copying the glassy ripples on the surface of the water. It was a good site for the colony. When the oyster had swum as a minute larva, its velum (projecting tissue that acts like a sail) lifted clear of its transparent shell and with its cilia stroking the water to give it direction, it found the boulder that was to be its

Opposite page:
These colourful cockscomb oysters are clinging to a rock by means of a limey secretion from the left mantlefold. They spend most of their adult lives in this way inside their hinged double shells. Members of the bivalvia class of molluscs, oysters lost their foot and the ability to move during the evolutionary process. Although a large foot, which is used in swimming, is present in the young oyster larvae, it shrinks so as to be almost non-existent when they finally become attached to a submerged object. Oysters are found in warm, temperate oceans throughout the world between the latitudes of 44°S and 64°N, usually in shallow, inshore waters which are diluted with fresh water from rivers and streams. However, most of the extensive oyster reefs have now disappeared as a result of pollution and over-fishing, and now they are farmed on a commercial basis.

These oysters, Crassostrea commercialis, *are being farmed along the coast of New South Wales, Australia, to supply seed pearls to manufacturing jewellery industries. Like other oysters in the* Crassostrea *genus, they are characterised by a deep left valve and, on the right side of the body, an irregularly shaped promyal chamber through which water from the right gill is discharged. Although the sexes are separate, they may change, and some species have both sets of reproductive organs in the same shell. Millions of eggs are discharged into the water by the oviparous oyster when spawning, many of which are eaten by predators and thus only a small percentage of the eggs survive as larvae.*

lifelong home. The bacteria from the decaying strands of eel grass had become its food.

The larva had swum for a while towards the light surface water, then, as it approached the rock, it withdrew its velum, closed its valves and sank away from the light. It dimly discerned the shadow of the overhang more than a metre below a tuft of seaweed that marked the highwater mark and opened its valves again to swim under the protection of the shallow lip of rock. The larva's foot, reaching upwards and forwards, had sought a hold on the boulder. It had fixed the tip of its foot to the hard surface. The muscle of the foot had contracted and the larva made a shuffling motion backwards and forwards as if it were 'treading itself in'. Quickly, it had squeezed out the sticky solution secreted in the gland at the root of its foot, cementing it for life to the rock it had chosen. Its spatfall (attachment) had been successfully accomplished and the development of the mature oyster could then take place.

Mysterious changes within the spat (immature oyster) had taken place. Its eyes had been ingested in a mere twenty-four hours. The foot had degenerated to leave only the horny threads that anchored the oyster to the rock. Organs and muscles within the animal's body had modified and moved to new positions and the shell had grown flatter and larger until its mature shape appeared. The crucial moment in its young life had passed without disaster. It might easily have gone wrong. The larva has only one chance of attachment. If it makes a bad choice of attachment site and comes unstuck, it will have no second chance to make spatfall and no chance of survival.

The young oyster had survived the rigours of one severe winter, when the harbour had borne a fringe of ice along its shores. The processes of its body had slowed down until the heartbeat had stopped. All that moved was the slowly swaying frill of cilia. Fortunately, the cold spell had not lasted long and the period of torpor did no serious and lasting damage to the young animal. That spring, the waters warmed its colourless blood and its heart again pumped at six or seven beats a minute.

The oyster had matured as a male. Shortly afterwards it had begun the slow change to its female phase and had spawned its first million eggs. Sperm clouds from other oysters in the colony had fertilised the eggs and the swarm of larvae had been safely discharged about eight days later. The sexual changes from female to male then followed more quickly. On this day, after the extreme low tide, the young oyster was in a female phase. The day before, she had liberated her eggs and passed them through the water tubes of her gills to the inhalant chamber of the mantle. There they lay like frost at the edges of her gills and lining the space just inside the margin of her shell. The sperm cloud that had puffed from those of the colony's oysters that were in their male phase had swept into the shell, on the current made by her waving cilia, and fertilised the eggs. Later, they would lose their shining whiteness and become grey; then they would turn purple, almost black, before the larvae would be ready to leave the shelter of the shell.

The tide was high when a five-armed shape of a pinkish colour, which looked unnatural in the grey-green water, swam among the rocks near the young oyster's anchorage. The red starfish pulsed slowly across the patch of eel grass and rummaged softly around the slipper limpet colony. Then it reached out the tip of a tentacle and delicately slipped it about the oyster's shell. The starfish settled onto the oyster without any hurry, shrugging itself into a position where it could exert pressure on the valves, its arms pointing towards the

This thorny oyster, Spondylus sp. *is so named because of the spines on its shell. Like other oysters, it breathes through a pair of gills situated under the mantle and consisting of two plates each of folded tubular filaments in a pleated effect. They pump water to provide the oyster with food and oxygen and ventilate the interior of the shell. They also play an important role in spawning, as eggs are discharged through the female's gill channels into the mantle before being deposited in the water.*

*Opposite page:
The common starfish,* Asterias rubens, *is a natural predator of the oyster, together with whelks, crabs, oystercatchers, fish and certain sea-snails. The oyster drill, a marine gastropod, is unusual in that it bores through the oyster's shell with its sharp tongue, which is covered with tiny teeth. Other snails insert their proboscis when the oyster opens its shell and suck out the blood. Many of these predators constitute a hazard to commercially farmed oysters as well as to those in the wild. Starfish have to be removed from oyster beds with special suction dredges and mops.*

This coral head is encrusted with hundreds of oysters, which are visible at low tide. Oysters have been regarded as a delicious food since Roman times and are now farmed specially for this purpose as well as to provide artificial pearls. The cultivation of oysters has been carried out for many centuries in artificial beds where the oysters are allowed to grow for about 18 months before being harvested and sorted. An oyster shell can be opened by running the point of a sharp knife around the edges of the hinged shell. The two halves are held together by a strong elastic ligament at the hinge and a central muscle.

oyster's hinge. The rows of tentacles snuggled into the most advantageous spots to exert pressure and the contest began.

The oyster's adductor had contracted hard, the quick muscle snapping the valves shut and the clutch muscle slowly locking the valves hard together. The starfish levered on its arms and the pressure rose. Soon, the leverage exerted a pressure on the oyster's shell equivalent to about three-and-a-half kilogrammes. Nothing moved. The starfish might have been resting.

After twenty minutes, a soft gleam appeared at the margin of the oyster's shell. The shiny strip of horny new shell parted a millimetre. Several minutes later, the gap opened to 12mm. The starfish opened its tiny mouth and its stomach of delicate membrane emerged and slipped between the parted valves. The starfish's digestive enzymes began to dissolve the mantle of the oyster. It was not necessary to tear open the oyster – a small opening of the valves was all that was required to end its life.

The meal over, the delicate pink shape of the starfish swam with exquisite langour towards the mouth of the harbour. The oyster's shell gaped open as the hinge ligament assumed its naturally straight position. The adductor muscle's stumps were still attached to the valves but had been torn apart in the middle.

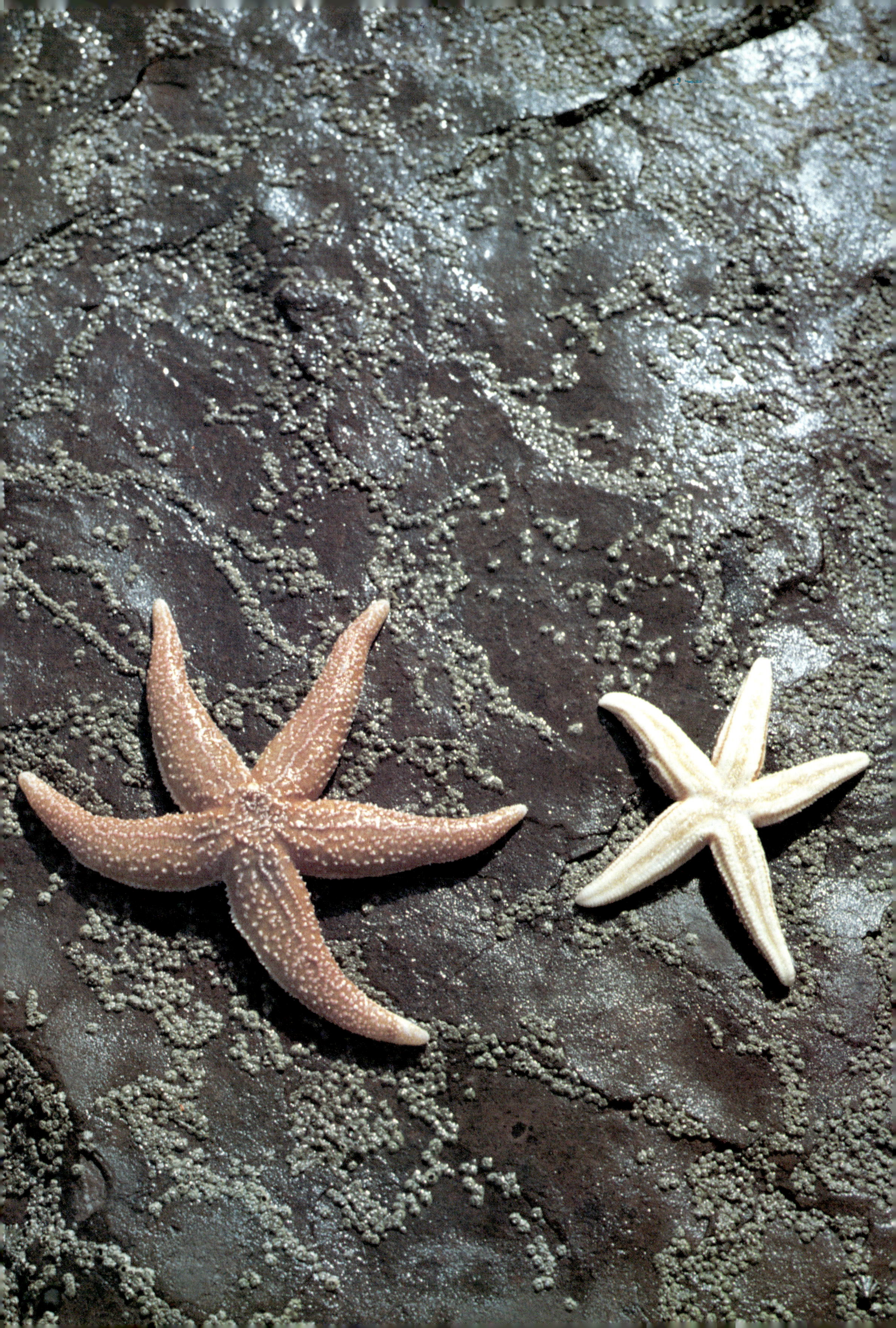

Crassostrea angulata

Pycnodonta hyotis

Ostrea edulis

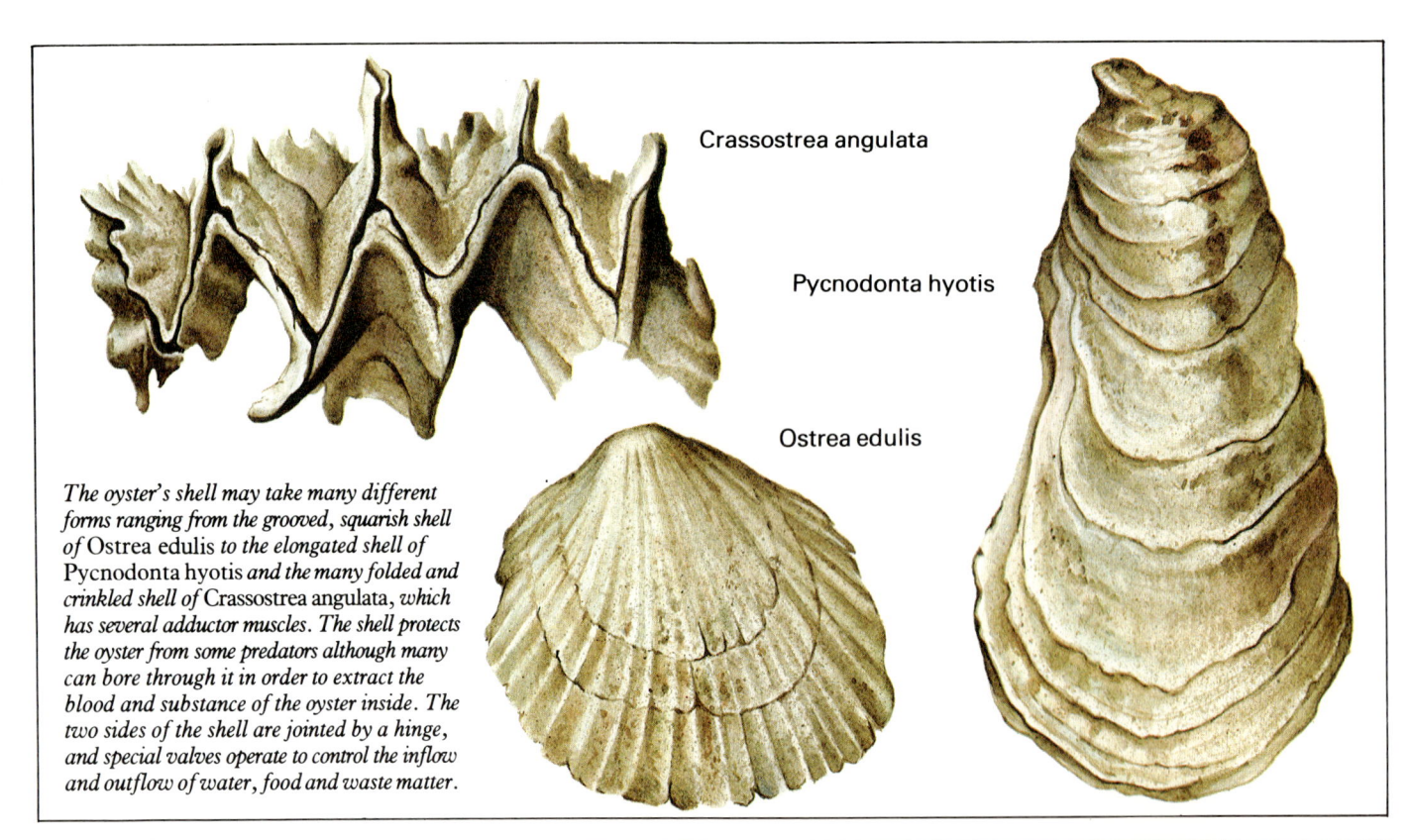

The oyster's shell may take many different forms ranging from the grooved, squarish shell of Ostrea edulis *to the elongated shell of* Pycnodonta hyotis *and the many folded and crinkled shell of* Crassostrea angulata, *which has several adductor muscles. The shell protects the oyster from some predators although many can bore through it in order to extract the blood and substance of the oyster inside. The two sides of the shell are jointed by a hinge, and special valves operate to control the inflow and outflow of water, food and waste matter.*

Species of oyster

The oyster's untidy shells hide one of the most extraordinary and intricate of nature's creations. It is a creature that is the product of extreme specialisation. It has evolved as a sedentary creature which creates the water eddies on which it depends. The currents carry its food through a delicately selective, filtering process for accepting or rejecting the foods drawn in through the opened valves of its shell. The oyster utilises its environment to this high degree of efficiency without the benefit of a true brain. By the time it reaches maturity, the oyster's nervous system consists of nothing more than a few ganglia (nerve centres), mainly centred in the middle fold of the edges of the mantle.

The three genera of true oysters - *Ostrea, Crassostrea* and *Pycnodonta* - inhabit shallow waters in all the polar seas. Even the *Pycnodonta* oysters do not venture into really deep water. All breed best in the temperate or warm conditions found along the continental shelves and in coral reefs. *Crassostrea* is most prolific in the warmer seas, and *Ostrea* thrusts into the cooler seas.

Man has had a considerable effect on the distribution of the oyster. Some naturalists believe that the Portuguese oyster was carried to the Mediterranean from warmer waters, perhaps clinging to the bottom of a ship, before breeding along the Portuguese and Spanish coasts. The move, if it happened in this way, must have occurred during the period of Roman domination of the area because shells of the species are found in association with second- and third-century discoveries. Much later, in our own century, man has begun to farm the marine resources provided by oyster beds, and he has experimented successfully with species foreign to his particular waters. The Portuguese oyster has been used to seed oyster beds in French and British waters, and the giant Japanese oyster has been introduced to American and British coasts with profitable results for the oystermen.

At the same time, the growing pollution of the seas around the mouths of the world's great rivers has threatened the existence of the natural beds as well as those made by man. The more concentrated conditions of growth required by the farming of molluscs, too, has created environments in which disease and massive predation can and do occur despite acute vigilance.

Several other bivalves are described as oysters but should be considered as members of separate families. The pearl oyster, saddle oyster and spiny, or thorny, oyster all have simpler gill structures, different ligament shapes and other arrangements for attaching themselves to rocks when compared with the true or edible oysters. They are more closely related to mussels than to oysters.

The **European oyster** (*Ostrea edulis*) is found in coastal waters of western Europe from the Mediterranean to latitude 65° north. See *At a glance* panel.

The **Pacific oyster** (*O. lurida*) inhabits the Pacific coast of North America from Alaska to California. Smaller than most oysters, it grows no longer than 7.5cm. It colonises the shore between the high and low water marks.

The **cockscomb oyster** (*O. crista galli*) is sometimes confused with the hyotoid oyster. It is smaller, and the zig-zag margins are more pronounced than the hyotoid's making it look like the cock's comb after which it is named. The shell of this oyster is thin and the animal lives in the tropical coastal waters of northern Australia, colonising rocks and coral below the low tide mark where it will never be uncovered.

O. mordax is a small oyster which inhabits the tidal zone of tropical Australian waters.

The **mud oyster** (*O. angasi*) lives in south-eastern Australian waters. A Stewart Island mud oyster from southern New Zealand may be of the same species. Some authorities place it in the species *O. chilensis*, which is native to the Chiloe Islands off southern Chile.

At a glance European oyster *Ostrea edulis*	
Class	Bivalvia
Order	Eulamellibranchia
Family	Ostreidae
Genus	Ostrea
Phylum	Mollusca
Eggs	In excess of 1,000,000 are discharged into the sea.
Incubation	Up to 14 days, depending on temperature.
Diet	Minute algae and micro-organisms.
Distribution	Western European coastal waters, including the Mediterranean Sea.

The New Zealand rock oyster (above) and the Atlantic thorny oyster (left) are very dissimilar in their appearance, the latter being more colourful. The rock oyster is found only along the shores and coastline of the North Island and is regarded as a delicacy by many gourmets.

The **Portuguese oyster** (*Crassostrea angulata*) colonises the eastern and southern seaboard of Portugal and Spain. Like all *Crassostrea* oysters it is long and deeply cupped in shape, and it does not incubate its eggs. Purple markings colour the outside of the shell and the points at which the adductor muscles are fixed are also purple. French and British oystermen cultivate the Portuguese oyster, although it does not often breed in the cooler waters of the English Channel.

The **American oyster** (*C. virginica*) is much like the Portuguese oyster in appearance and other characteristics. It grows to *c*.15.5cm. There are several varieties, of which the most celebrated among gourmets is the blue point. This type has a deeply cupped lower valve and is more rounded than most. It will spawn between 15 million and 115 million eggs at a time, several times a year.

The **Japanese oyster** (*C. gigas*) occurs naturally around the coasts of Japan and Korea, but the species has also been farmed successfully in the Pacific waters of Canada and North America and along the coast of Australia. It is even grown in some sheltered harbours of Europe. As its name suggests, it grows to a great length, over 31cm in some specimens. It spawns up to 60 million eggs at a time and may repeat this process several times a year.

C. rivularis, C. nippona, and **C. echinata** are three other of the 14 species of *Crassostrea* found in the waters of Japan. *Rivularis* is smaller and rounder than the Japanese giant oyster, and is found along the west coast and in some Korean waters.

C. margaritacea is the most abundant oyster of the southern African coasts and is found from the Cape of Good Hope to Madagascar. Another common African species is the *C. gasar*, which is found on the tidal zone from Senegal to Angola.

The oystercatcher is a wading bird found on the sea-shores of all continents except Antarctica. Its long, compressed bill is perfectly adapted for opening and smashing the shells of shellfish, including oysters, mussels and other bivalves. It pulls the tightly closed shells off the rocks and oyster beds, hammers a hole in the flat surface of the shell and cuts through the adductor muscle, securing the two halves of the shell fast and together. Using its bill as a lever, the oystercatcher then prises the two halves of the shell apart and extracts the meat within. They also feed on worms.

The **common rock oyster** (*C. cucullata*) inhabits the coastal waters of India and east Africa and the eastern Mediterranean. It is barely distinguishable from the rock oyster of New Zealand (*C. glemerata*) and from *C. commercialis*. The New Zealand rock oyster colonises the shores of the north island of New Zealand, and *C. commercialis* is found round the Australian coasts except for the southern area.

O. denselamellosa is a deep-water oyster that can succeed in waters of fairly high salinity. It lives in small numbers off the coast of Japan.

The **crested oyster** (*O. equestris*), the leafy or coon oyster (*O. frons*) and *O. permollis* all live along the southern seaboard of the United States and on the shores of the West Indies. The first two have processes on their underparts that enable them to hold on to corals or other stem-like objects. Their outer margins are zig-zagged. *O. permollis* attaches itself to sponges. All three oysters are small.

The **hyotoid oyster** (*Pycnodonta hyotis*) lives in the Atlantic, Indian and Pacific oceans in waters as deep as 90m. It is fairly common on coral reefs, such as the Australian Great Barrier and the pair of shells alone can weigh up to 3.18kg. The hyotoid oyster does not incubate its eggs but rejects them as soon as they have been fertilised. Unlike other genera, the *Pycnodonta* do not colonise to form reefs.

The **mangrove oyster** (*C. rhizophorae*) lives in the West Indies.

55

Anatomy

The oyster shell is in the form of two valves, or sides. When at rest, the European oyster lies on its deeply cupped left valve. The material of the shell is formed by the general surface of the mantle (the fleshy lining of each valve). The mantle separates into three folds at its edges. The inner surface of the outer mantle fold secretes a thin, organic, horny layer called the periostracum. This layer covers the whole shell and the ligaments but soon wears away. Beneath it are two layers of conchyolin, the horny, hard material that incorporates calcium from the sea water. The oyster produces an enzyme, phosphatase, which enables the conchyolin to convert the sea water's calcium into calcium carbonate in these two layers of its shell.

The inner layer of shell, the mother-of-pearl material, is a crystalline form of calcium called aragonite. The middle layer is of another crystalline form of calcium called calcium carbonate. The periostracum is slightly elastic, uniting the edge of the mantle to the outer surface of the shell, so that the folds of the mantle can be withdrawn from the margin of the shell when the valves close. Chalky deposits in the shell act as padding, and there may be chambers in the shell walls. These chambers are filled with water and putrifying matter which gives off a rotten eggs smell (sulphurated hydrogen). These gaps in the valve walls are the consequence of the mantle surface shrinking, perhaps due to changes in the salinity of the water.

The oyster can operate the inner folds (velum) of the mantle, dropping the upper one and raising the lower one to seal off the oyster from an inrush of debris, food particles that are too large or an unwanted inflow of water. This is an important feeding mechanism. The mantle's middle fold is equipped with minute sensory organs leading to a nerve that runs along the mantle margin. The sense organs are sited on small tentacles, and are chemico-receptive, like those of taste and smell in mammals. It is possible that they may also react to light and salinity changes. The ligament consists of the same material as that of the valves it joins, but is less completely calcified. The ligament is in its 'correct' shape when the valves are apart, and is misshapen when the valves are closed by the contraction of the big adductor muscle. This muscle has two parts, the catch muscle and the quick muscle. The fibres of these two vary. Those of the catch muscle operate slowly and retain the pull for long periods, while the quick muscle operates swiftly and tires rapidly. The catch muscle is noticeably well developed in oysters that are exposed by the tide, and which have to remain tightly shut for long periods.

Reproduction

The sex of the oyster alternates between male and female throughout its life. Most young oysters are male when they mature sexually. Then they undergo a slow change to a female phase, after which the phases alternate more rapidly. The change from male to female functions takes a few weeks, depending on the temperature and richness of the waters. The switch back to male takes only a few days after the eggs have been discharged.

Spawning takes place throughout the

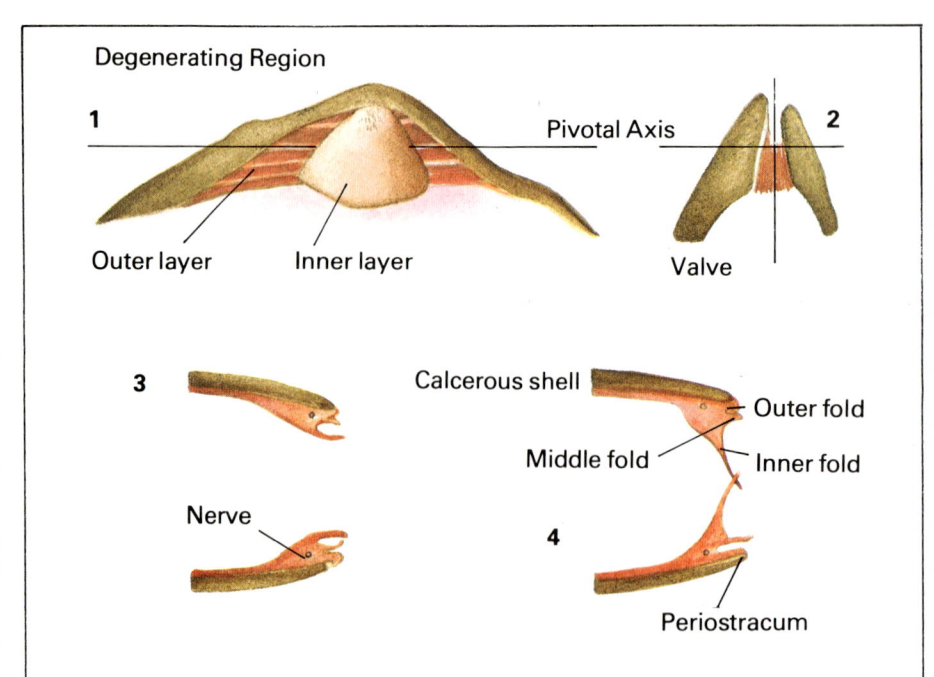

The ligament of a young oyster is viewed above as it is in the right valve (1) and as the transverse section through the inner layer (2). A diagrammatic representation of the nerve is shown (3) and a section through the edges of the open shell valves (4). In (4), in order to prevent the passage of water the inner valves are extended. When the oyster opens the valves, unwanted water and faeces are shot clear of its shell and then the valves snap shut.

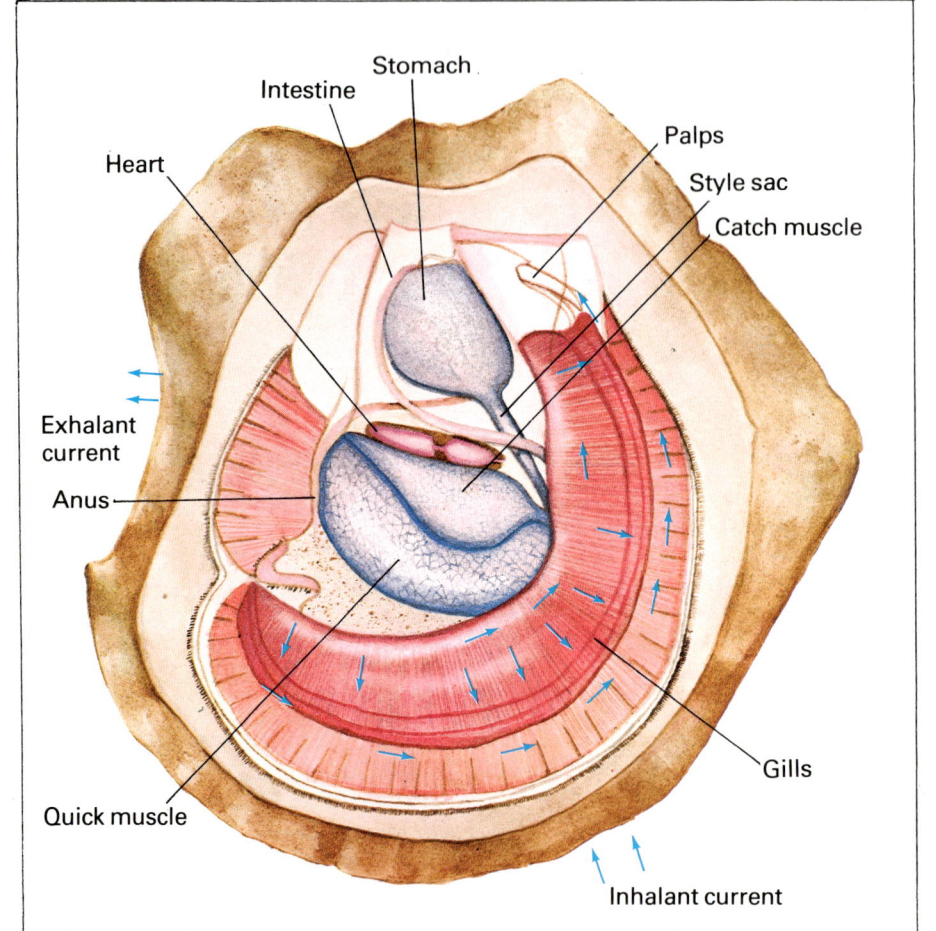

This cross-section through an oyster shows its internal organs. The small arrows indicate the direction of the feeding currents along the gills and palps during the digestive process. Digestive waste is excreted through the exhalant chamber. The broad arrows indicate the direction of the inhalant and exhalant currents as the oyster's respiratory system functions. On the gills are hair-like organs called cilia which wave to produce a flow of water through the inhalant chamber and the gills themselves.

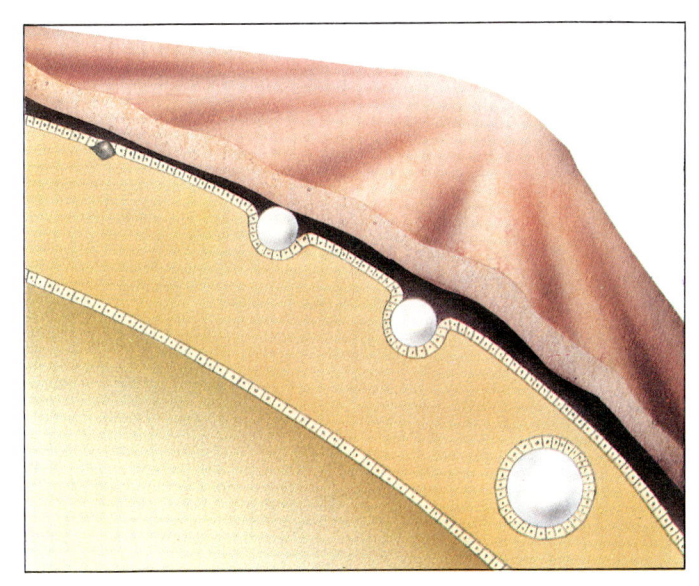

Oysters are now cultivated extensively in many parts of the world on special oysters farms. This is not a new phenomenon and dates back to ancient Roman times. This oyster farm (above left) is in New South Wales, Australia, the oysters being bred in large beds. Over-fishing of traditional oyster grounds has led to the widespread establishment of such farms where oysters can be protected from predators and disease. In this way, oysters can be farmed as a food and also to provide pearls for industry. The diagram (above right) shows how a pearl is formed inside the shell of the oyster and the various stages in its development. Cultured pearls are produced by introducing artificially a foreign object into the shell of the mollusc. The Chinese discovered this technique in the thirteenth century and it was later perfected by the Japanese. Cultured pearls inside the shells are shown (right) before their removal to be made into jewellery.

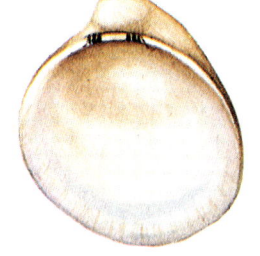

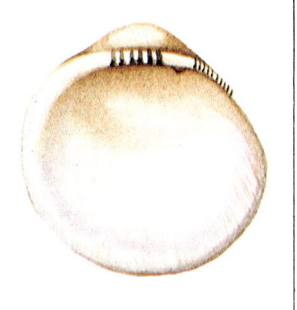

Ostrea edulis   Crassostrea angulata   Pycnodonta hyotis

These are the late larval shells of three genera of oysters, showing both the hinge teeth and ligaments. The shell of Ostrea edulis has a ligament inside the plate's end and two teeth at each end of the hinge. Crassostrea angulata's ligament is outside the hinge plate and has two teeth at each end. Five teeth are arranged equally along the hinged plate of Pycnodonta hyotis with 10 teeth arranged along the valve margins.

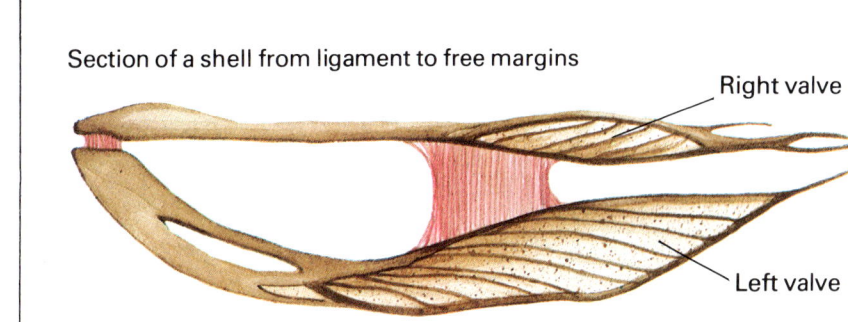

Section of a shell from ligament to free margins

Right valve

Left valve

This is a section through an old oyster shell from a natural bed in the cold waters of the North Sea. Viewed from the ligament to the free margins, the shell has a noticeable chamber in the lower valve. Horny, prismatic scales are visible in the right valve's upper edge. Much of the shell is made up of a hard layer joined by the two valves.

summer. The European oyster requires a temperature of over 15° for spawning. The eggs are discharged into the exhalant cavity, and drawn through the water tubes into the inhalant cavity. When the neighbouring oyster emits a cloud of sperm, the oyster in its female phase draws in the sperm solution which then fertilises the eggs. The oyster retains them for about eight days before releasing the larvae.

After fertilisation, the egg divides repeatedly into clusters of cells. The embryo becomes a hollow sphere and one side becomes slightly flattened. A tuft of cilia grows at one end, a larval shell at the other. In good, warm waters the fifth day sees the animal fully encased in its two valves.

For about two-and-a-half weeks, the larvae drift with other minute animals and plants as part of the plankton feeding on plant cells of up to one-hundredth of a millimetre in length. In this period they triple their volume, and grow to three-tenths of a millimetre long.

A foot develops with a retractor muscle. At the base of the foot is situated a byssus gland which can open a duct oozing a viscous fluid. The substance sets as a horny thread in water. By the time the larvae are ready to attach themselves, over 90 per cent of the original swarm will have perished. The survivors will have developed eyes within their shells, which are still transparent. They move upwards towards light and then seem to search out a shady place. They attach themselves by means of their feet, sticking themselves in place with the sticky threads produced by byssus glands. The act of attachment is called 'spatfall', and the larvae become 'spat'. Their shells flatten out and grow longer, giving them better attachment and less water resistance.

The larva's eyes disappear the day after spatfall. The foot and vellum also degenerate, leaving the thread to hold the spat in place.

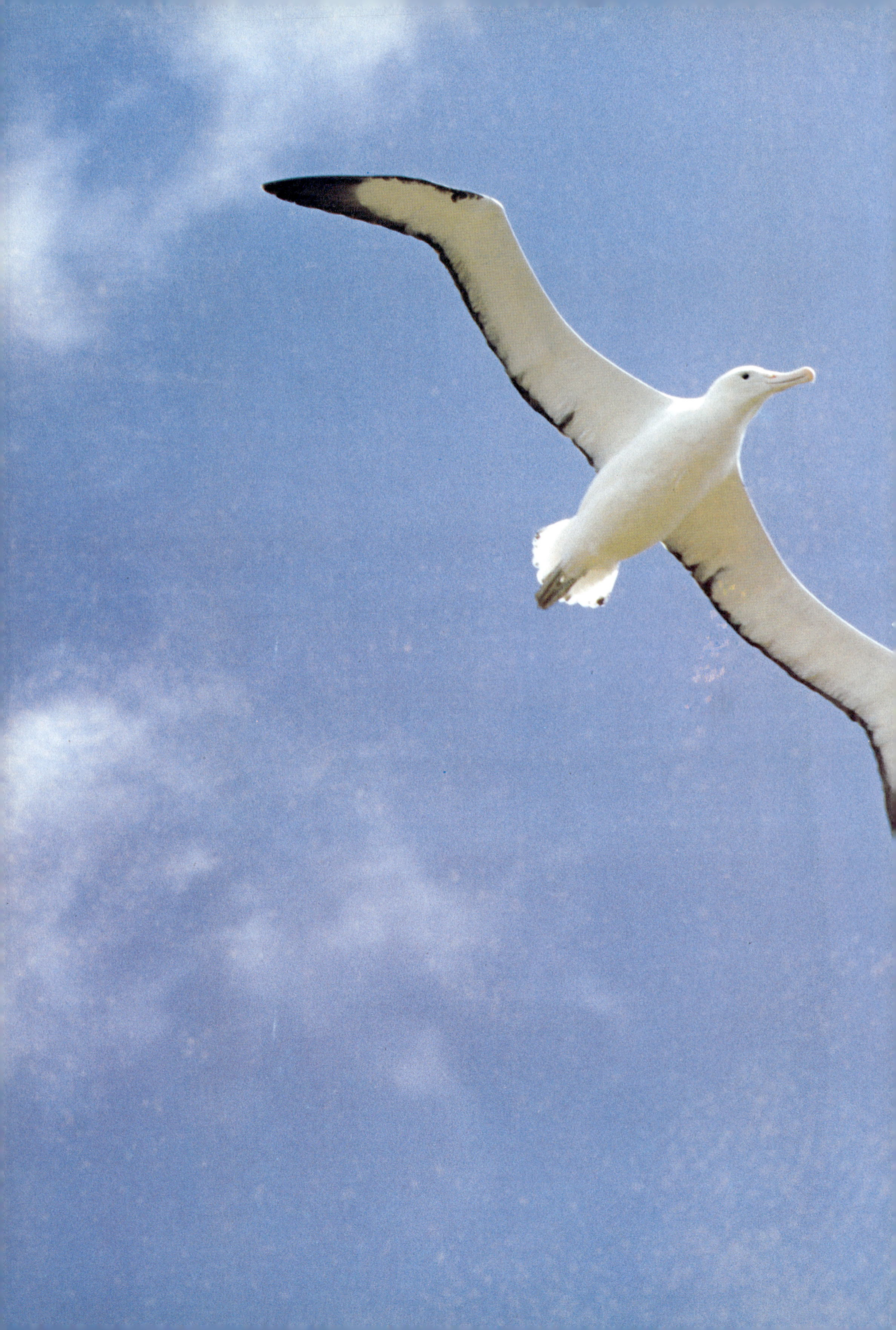

The Albatross

A world of uncertainty: of milky dampness with airy and watery space mingled in a chilly fog. A wind that was scarcely more than a draught of cold air stirred and rearranged the banks of pale vapour, lifting them a little above the long swell that rolled shorewards. The pale sun gradually drew up the fog and thinned it out to leave a wedge of clearer air between the gently heaving sea and the cloud-dimmed sky. Far away, a grey and white shape planed across the waves, zig-zagging towards the coast.

The female royal albatross rose slowly as she met the thermals above the beach and looked down at the curious sight below. The ground was pocked with small cones, each supporting a fluffy, white albatross. It looked rather like a series of small volcanoes with the plump 60-day old hatchlings sitting on top of them. The female curved in to make her landing.

Up to the moment she turned into the wind, her wings remained still except for slight adjustments to their angles as they steered her home. As she made her approach, she tilted her body and stretched out her feet, toes up, flapped hard and used her wings to reduce speed. She thumped into the grassy headland and scored twin tracks in the soft turf with her heels, bouncing into the air again with wings spread wide, frantically banging the ground to keep her balance. Finally, she tilted forwards and stumbled to a halt while resting on her broad white breast. The landing had been nerve-rackingly accomplished.

She waddled forwards, pausing to sort out some of her disarranged breast feathers, and walked between the steep-sided mounds that supported the colony's nests. The other birds watched her without concern as she approached a nest guarded by a large male. His head appeared to wear a less alert expression than his mate's; perhaps her more profuse cap of dark feathers lent her features greater contrast.

The youngster in the nest opened its bill hungrily and, after a brief greeting, the female opened her bill to allow her offspring to eat the food she regurgitated. From time to time, the female drew away from her hatchling and preened her plumage while her mate watched companionably. Soon he grew restless, walking around the nest mound until finally he moved away. As he left the nests he faced into the onshore breeze and spread his great wings. The weak sunlight shone on them and reflected the sheen from their well preened surfaces. He began to run forwards, his stride growing longer as his speed increased. Great flaps of his wings sent him lurching into the air, but despite his efforts he could not find enough 'lift' to draw himself fully into his element. The take-off petered out in an undignified stagger and he walked disconsolately around for some minutes. The wind freshened and seemed to encourage him to make another try. This time he strode into it until the strides became wild hops, and at last he drove himself into the air. With a few beats of his wings he rose above the shore, tilted on one wing, and curved out in a long glide over the grey sea.

He circled back close to the land, and as he flew near the nest the female threw up her head until it was nearly vertical and uttered a few musical notes of a sweet sound. As she finished her sky-call to her mate she lowered her head and stretched out her bill parallel to the ground. She stayed still for nearly a minute before moving to her chick again.

The male banked steeply across the blue-grey sky and swooped to wave level. He began his zig-zag path out to sea. His flight seemed carelessly easy, tilting his way along the troughs of waves and then rising through the updraughts above the wavetops to soar nearly 100 m up into the air before planing down again to within a few metres of the sea. For more than an hour he steered his way through the brisk wind, making delicate adjustments to the profile of his wings, flexing the long black-fringed flight feathers and angling the wing surfaces to make speed or gain lift from the element that was his true home.

After his first flight from the nesting ground when he had been a yearling, he had spent just over six years without alighting on any land – six years of learning the ways of the winds and the oceans. The lesson had barely been necessary as flying was instinctive to him anyway and the only testing times had come when the winds had gone mad and rushed along at over 150 kilometres an hour and the sea spray had been like a wall of suffocating water. Then, all his sensitive skill had helped him to skim through the shelter of the wave troughs and to sit out the worst of the storm on the sea itself.

Now, the wind gathered force across the broad swell and rose to 65 kilometres an hour. He swung through beautiful arcs, dipping and climbing along a course towards the distant feeding grounds where the ocean was rich with food. As he swept through the spray-laden air, a stream of drops flew from the oval openings in the upper member of his bill. These drops of concentrated salt solution sprayed away from his bill, missing the sensitive skin around his

Opposite page:
These royal albatrosses are mating after performing their mutual courtship display which consists of an elaborate ritual of wing-flapping, bowing and raucous screams, croaks and groans. These displays continue throughout the breeding season between mated pairs of birds. A single egg is laid and the chick emerges after an incubation period of up to 79 days to be cared for by its parents.

One of the largest species of albatrosses, the royal albatross is perfectly adapted to its way of life — gliding effortlessly over the vast expanses of the southern oceans, where strong wind currents provide lift for these graceful birds. It is a stoutly built bird with long, narrow wings, and short legs with webbed toes which make it appear very clumsy on land. It spends most of its life at sea but nests on oceanic islands during the breeding season in huge colonies of thousands of birds. At sea, it follows the trade winds and seems to navigate by the prevailing winds and the sun and stars. In fact, even if it is many thousands of kilometres from its breeding area and nest, it can return there quickly with little effort. It lives on fish, crustaceans and any fatty, oily foods.

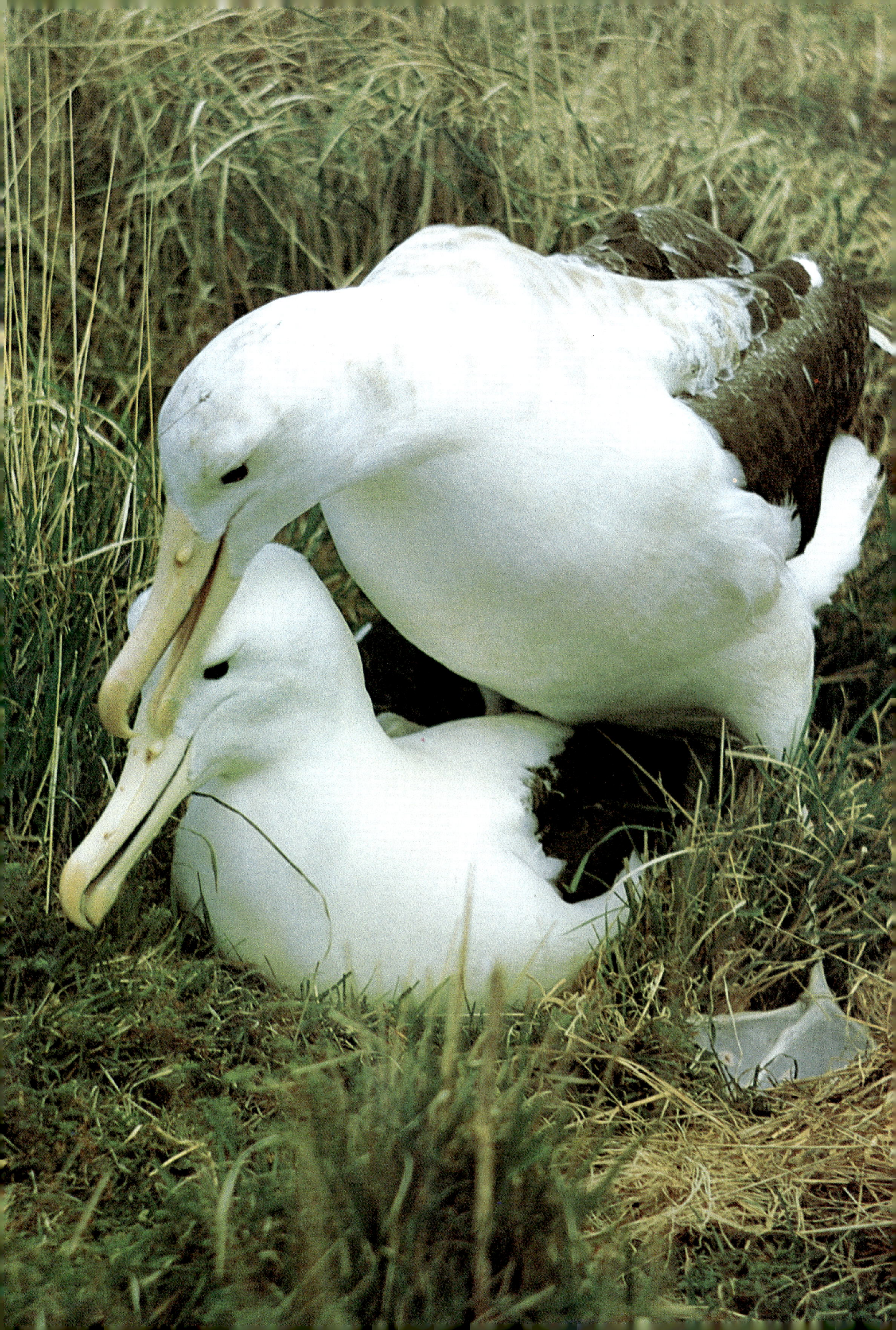

This royal albatross male is displaying to a watching female during the breeding season which lasts from September to January — the southern spring. With neck arched aesthetically and beak pointing skywards, he flaps his wings and performs enthusiastically. The black-browed albatrosses (opposite) are preening each other.

eyes. When feeding, he might take in nearly a tenth of his bodyweight of salt water, and the glands in his skull, a little below his eyes, would concentrate the salts, and the solution would drip from the bird's bill. In three hours, 90 percent of the salt would have left the albatross's body, leaving nearly fresh water to help its digestion and keep its organs moist.

The flight was a long one. Over 900 kilometres from the nest site, he flew closer to the waves, searching with sharp eyes. The light was going, and with the oncoming darkness the sea creatures that lived deep in the ocean began to rise towards the surface. They glimmered with phosphorescence, and the albatross used its wings to slow down for a landing. The great bird splashed into the glassy sea and plunged its bill deep into the water to take a good-sized squid. The black edged, razor-sharp rims of the bill grasped the slippery creature, and the bird tossed it lightly around so that it could swallow the meal. Powerful gastric juices would digest most of the squid, but its beak might stay in the albatross's stomach for many months.

While the male bird was stocking itself with food to restore its own strength and to bring back a reserve for the hatchling, the mother bird had flown off a little way to look for more morsels for the hungry youngster. For some minutes, the colony was unusually clear of adult birds – most of them were collected around the lowest part of the colony. It was at this time that the rakish silhouette of a great skua darted towards the unguarded nests. As soon as the youngsters saw the predator they recognised the danger. The powerful skua landed close to the unfledged bird whose mother had recently left it. The fluffy plump nestling pointed her bill at the skua and began to snap. Its bill was long, hooked at the tip and threatening. As the skua approached warily, the albatross suddenly spat a jet of liquid that struck the skua's breast feathers. From a nearby nest, another baby albatross ejected a similar jet of pinkish liquid towards the skua.

The skua backed off hastily. There was an unpleasant musky

The chicks of the black-browed albatross have little in common with their parents' good looks. A single pink and white speckled egg is laid in the spring and the chick is born after 56-79 days in a nest of grass and mud. These chicks live in a large colony on West Point Island in the Falklands group in the southern Atlantic Ocean. The black-browed albatross is found in the southern seas from the Tropic of Capricorn to 60° south. It feeds on fish, crustaceans and squid and regurgitates these to feed a hungry chick. It is a favourite bird of sailors and follows ships, often for many days at a time, closer than any other albatross.

smell in the air, and the liquid quickly congealed on the bird's feathers, leaving a waxy deposit that clotted them. The young albatrosses were still spitting and snapping when the mother bird rose above the headland to make her landing. The skua took off with long slow beats of his wings and fled to a safe place where he could preen his feathers clean.

On the lower part of the island shore, as the afternoon wore on, three young albatrosses watched a party of five others wheeling and banking above them. Occasionally the musical notes of the sky-calls sang out, but the birds on the ground seemed to be mostly interested in rubbing bills against one another. The airborne birds flew about the billing birds that stood on the turf. Another well-grown albatross wandered across to join the ground party. These were mature albatrosses that had not yet bred successfully, and in the party in the air was a pair that had lost their chick to a skua a few weeks earlier.

The visiting bird followed two of the albatrosses away from the party to bill with them, but the paired male turned on him and made an aggressive noise by clappering his bill together so rapidly that the lower part of it became a blur. The visitor took the hint and rejoined the main party.

The young couple sat quietly for half an hour, watching the ground party billing and rubbing necks. The young male pointed his bill towards the sky and, opening it slightly, made a curious yapping sound while his head moved gently up and down. He leaned over and preened his partner's feathers. After caressing her for some time, he moved around to face her. He stretched out his head and lay his bill for a moment along her shoulder feathers.

Slowly he drew back, his bill still pointing towards her, and began to swing his head from side to side as he made a noise rather like the whinnying of a pony. He began to extend his long narrow wings while rising up on his toes. His tail fanned out and rose up, and his breast puffed out while the whinny continued.

While he so displayed, the female stood still, her head pushed forward awkwardly. Gradually, the male raised his head until it pointed to the sky. He could no longer swing his head from side to side in this position and he lowered his heels to the ground to stand flat-footed again. He stopped the whinnying and broke into the call he had used earlier when crying to the albatrosses wheeling in the sky above his head. The musical notes rang through the late afternoon air and the young nestlings turned their heads to listen. When he had called for a little over a minute in this way, he walked closer to the female and they both sat down, remaining quietly together for an hour.

The mother bird, returning to her fledgeling, made a sky-call, similar to that of the displaying male, and fed her young. Out across the darkening sea, her lifelong mate began to glide his way back to the breeding ground. The offspring would soon have a large meal again; an unusually short period between feasts, she often waited several days for a feed. The adults often had searched further afield before returning with full crops to the nests. For many more weeks they would keep up their care for the young bird until it had grown its long flight feathers. About 236 days after it emerged from the white egg, with its speckled pointed end, the young albatross would stretch out its wings and stagger across the turf to launch itself into its home, the windy wastes that stretch for endless leagues around the southern hemisphere.

The ungainly albatross chicks are fed by their parents until they are old enough to fly. This fledging period may last for several months until the young bird is ready to leave the nest and take its first uncertain flight. Although this usually takes about five months, a record eight and a half month period has been recorded for a royal albatross. The chick is fed less frequently by its parents as time passes and is left to fend for itself for increasingly long periods. If molested by a predatory skua, it will vomit the unpleasant, oily contents of its stomach at its enemy, often with great accuracy, and this acts as an effective deterrent.

Species of albatross

There are 13 species of albatrosses. They are grouped in the order *Procellariiformes* (tube-nosed birds), which has a history stretching back in time to the Upper Eocene period (about 30 million years ago — in the Old World). No one knows the population numbers of these birds living in the world today. Counting such lonely voyagers is obviously nearly impossible. One of the species, the short-tailed albatross, was thought by many ornithologists of the 1940s to be extinct, but happily a relic population still exists, breeding on an isolated island off the southern tip of Japan.

Albatrosses were once fairly common in the Atlantic Ocean, but now are seen there only on rare occasions. Most live and breed south of the Tropic of Capricorn in the isolation of the world's richest and loneliest seas. Here, the winds blow almost constantly, giving the birds the motive power essential to their gliding flight. A few sightings of albatrosses, usually the large wandering albatross, have been made as far north as the 60th parallel of latitude: dramatic evidence of the birds' amazing capacities as long-distance fliers.

The **white-capped albatross** (*D. cauta*) breeds on the islands off New Zealand and Tasmania. Its feeding grounds extend as far as the east and west coasts of South America. The bird's white cap is highlighted by dark bands that run above the eyes, and by the grey neck feathers. Its underwing is white with narrow black rims and with a broad black tip. The bird's legs are bluish-grey, and its bill is yellow on the upper ridge, merging to a pinkish brown. The white-capped albatross does not fly as far from land as most others of the family. It lays its eggs in September.

The **short-tailed albatross** (*Diomedea albatrus*) is the rarest of the albatrosses. It is entirely white when adult, but as a nestling it is dark brown, giving it better camouflage on or near the nest. The female lays her eggs in October or November, and the young birds fly in June.

Buller's albatross (*D. bulleri*) breeds on isolated islands off the coast of New Zealand, and flies as far as the Peruvian current in search of food. Its white underwing has a narrow black edge, but its back and the upper surface of the wings are sooty brown. It has pale grey cheeks and neck, and a white forehead. The bird's underparts are white. The body of the Buller's albatross is about 81.25cm long, and it has a wingspan of 2.43m.

The **Galapagos albatross** (*D. irrorata*) breeds on the island of Espanola in the Galapagos group. This is the only known nesting site for the bird, and observers estimate that only about 2,000 pairs breed there. The Galapagos variety is the only tropical albatross.

The **black-browed albatross** (*D. melanophris*) is hard to distinguish from the yellow-nosed in flight, but close observation shows that the black margins on the underwings are broader in the black-browed variety. Its bill is yellow, and the bird has a characteristic dark streak across the area of the eye. Its body is about one metre long, and its wingspan is between 2.25m and 2.75m. Black-browed albatrosses breed on the Aukland, Campbell and Falkland islands and south of latitude 50° on the west coast of South America. It is an ocean wanderer and is found as far north as the 60th parallel.

The **grey-headed albatross** (*D. chrysostoma*) breeds on the Campbell, Kerguelen and Diego Ramirez Islands, and at Cape Horn and South Georgia. It fishes the seas off the coasts of Argentina and Chile, and the Australian waters around Shark Bay and New South Wales. The bird's head is a pale lavender-grey and there is a patch of white behind each eye. The undersides of the wings are white except for the black tips of the feathers. Its bill is blackish-grey with a yellow line along the ridge of the upper mandible and a band of the same colour at the base of the lower one. The tip of the upper mandible is reddish-orange. Young grey-headed albatrosses have uniformly black bills and only aquire the yellow markings as they mature. Their plumage is dark too and lightens with age. An adult is about 91.5cm long.

The **yellow-nosed albatross** (*D. chlororhynchos*) is slightly smaller than the black-browed albatross, but in flight looks similar. The yellow-nosed albatross breeds on Tristan da Cunha and Gough Island, and ranges as far north as the Brazilian and Argentinian coasts. It has white underwings, edged by narrow black markings, and its bill is black with a yellow streak along the top and an orange tip.

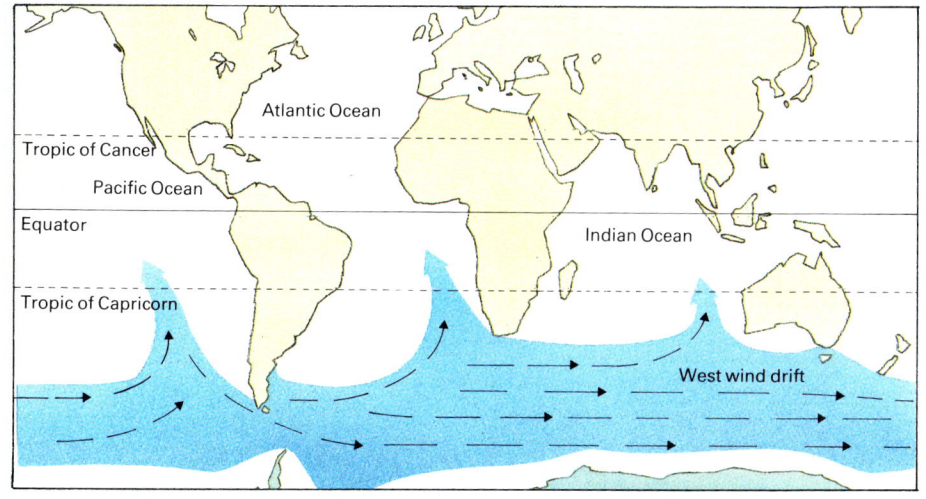

Some of the different species of albatross are shown above, including the largest, the wandering albatross, which has the widest wing-span of any bird (up to 3.5m). The light mantled and sooty albatrosses are two species of Phoebetria, which are distinguished from the Diomedea *albatrosses by their dark plumage, narrow wings and white eye rings. Their narrow wings make them the most graceful and accomplished fliers of all the albatrosses, especially when combined with their lightness and manoeuvrability. They tend to nest on cliff ledges and in inaccessible places, which can be approached only from the air.*

The bird's body is about 75cm long and it has a wingspan of 2-2.25m. The yellow-nosed albatross is more gregarious than most other members of the family and is quite often seen in small groups at sea.

The **royal albatross** (*D. exulans*) See *At a Glance* panel.

The **black-footed albatross** (*D. nigripes*) breeds on islands of the northern Pacific Ocean. US authorities, concerned about the number of collisions between aircraft and black-footed albatrosses, tried to eradicate them around the airbase on Midway Island. Their numbers are estimated at a healthy 300,000 birds, despite this declaration of war.

The **wandering albatross** (*D. exulans*) breeds in various sub-Antarctic islands, and is the most far-ranging of all the family. It is seen throughout the southern seas as far north as the Tropic of Capricorn; exceptionally, this wanderer has been seen as far north as the North Sea. It has a white face and throat when young, but becomes mainly white with black wingtips when adult. A pair incubates a single egg for about 76 days before hatching, and care for the hatchlings for a minimum of 220 days before the young birds fly. The egg size is, on average, 127 x 80mm and weighs about 458g; an exceptional egg was found to weigh 588g, but such a size is rare.

The wandering albatross is the largest of the family, and has a greater wingspan than any other bird. Males average 3m, and the females slightly less, from wing tip to wing tip, but the largest male ever measured had a wingspan of 3.6m. The bird's 20cm bill is yellow or pinkish with a yellow tip. Its body is about 128cm long, and the bird weighs, on average, 8.18kg, but a very large specimen weighed 16.13kg.

The **sooty albatross** (*D. fusca*) breeds on Tristan de Cunha and Gough Island, and ranges over the southern seas. It has a black bill, whose lower mandible is marked by a yellow groove. Its body is 82cm long. Some naturalists classify this bird as a member of a separate family, Phoebetria.

The **Laysan albatross** (*D. immutabilis*) is one of three species of albatross that are generally found in seas of the northern hemisphere. The other two species are the short-tailed and the black-footed albatrosses.

The **light-mantled sooty albatross** (*D. palpebrata*) is now classified by some ornithologists as a member of another family, the *Phoebetria*. It is one of the most graceful flyers of all albatrosses. It has a black bill with a purple groove on the lower mandible. Its plumage is grey or greyish-brown, and it has an incomplete ring of white round each eye. The light-mantled sooty albatross has a body of about 71cm long and a wingspan of about 1.8m. It breeds on islands to the south of New Zealand, and on Kerguelen Island and South Georgia.

The champion glider

No modern sailplane, incorporating man's strongest and lightest materials, the most advanced aerodynamic design and flown by an accomplished glider pilot, can equal the performance of an albatross in flight. The bird's narrow, long wings and streamlined body make it the most perfect glider in the world. Without even flapping its wings, it can sail through the air for over an hour at a time before a graceful sweep of its wings adds an extra lift.

The aspect-ratio, the relationship between wing width and wing length, of an advanced glider's wing is about 18, the same as that of an albatross. However, the bird has one advantage that is impossible to transfer to a man-made wing; it can alter its wing's profile and modify its width and length in flight by extending and retracting the feathers, or the 'arm' bones, that support the flight surface. The bird can adjust the angle also between its body and the forward edge of the wing. This flexibility in usage, and also the length and narrowness of its wings, makes the albatross's wings ideal for their function of sustained oceanic flight.

The bird's body, like that of other fliers, is well supplied with air sacs and is constructed on a skeleton of hollow bones. An albatross of 10kg would have a skeleton weighing no more than 1.5kg, including the bill, legs and feet.

The albatross's motive power is the wind, and in the Antarctic waters, unlike the Atlantic Ocean which has periods of calm, the air is rarely still. The gliding bird uses a combination of gravity, updraught from the waves and the driving force of the wind currents. As the wind blows across the sea, it is slowed down by friction with the surface. This effect is greater at a height of a few centimetres above the surface than it is higher up. This effect helps a bird that is diving to pick up a greater air-speed than if the air were moving at a constant rate at all heights. Thus, when it tilts its wings to climb again, the resistance of air under the wings gives it a lot more lift.

The updraught from the waves gives the albatross an extra drive upwards into the air, and the bird uses these lifting currents of air and the volumes of calmer airs that lie in the troughs of the waves to help it maintain its mean course. The characteristic flight pattern of the albatross is a series of flat-topped zig-zags rising and falling. The stronger the wind, the narrower the deviations from the mean course needs to be.

A way with salt water

Albatrosses, like other seabirds, take in a great deal of salt water when eating and fishing. Their bodies have evolved a way of ridding themselves of excess salt. If they retained the salt, then they would be forced to lose large quantities of water and would die of dehydration.

The order of *Procellariiformes* (tube-nosed birds) are equipped with a pair of nasal glands that open into the bill, with exits through a pair of round, or oval, holes. These glands operate rather like an extra kidney, but they are more specialised, being able to secrete sodium, chlorine and water with minute amounts of potassium. The secretions pass out of the bird through the nasal openings in its bill.

The albatross makes use of the prevailing winds by zig-zagging, in the manner of a ship tacking, through the sky, climbing and descending in winds of varying strength. The broad blue ribbon shows the rise and fall and direction of the albatross's flight path as it glides above the ocean. The arrows indicate the direction of the winds it encounters. The winds are slowed down by friction with the surface of the sea, and thus the albatross has to rise and dive alternately to pick up a greater air speed and to make use of lift and allow for drag. Deviations from the bird's main course are less in strong than in light winds.

At a glance
Royal albatross
Diomedea epomophora

Class	Aves
Order	Procellariiformes
Family	Diomedea
Genus	Epomophora
Body length	1.07-1.22m
Wingspan	3.35m approximately
Weight	7-8.5kg
Egg	One egg is laid in alternate years. It is white or cream with reddish spots at the narrower end.
Incubation	79 days
First flight	At about 236 days old.
Lifespan	Generally 30-40 years. The oldest recorded was 47 years.
Breeding sites	Sub-Antarctic islands and the Otago Peninsula in New Zealand.
Range	The southern seas to the Tropic of Capricorn in the north, and even further along the Humbolt current.
Food	Fish, crabs, squid, other seabirds, penguins and scraps from ships' refuse.

Royal albatross   Sky albatross

These dorsal views show the skulls of the sky and royal albatrosses. The long, elongated bill has internal horny tubes in the nostril openings as in the tube-nosed order of birds. Separate horny plates make up the bill covering, and the hooked end of the upper mandible is used for grasping slippery fish and other food when fishing by sitting on the water or diving onto its prey.

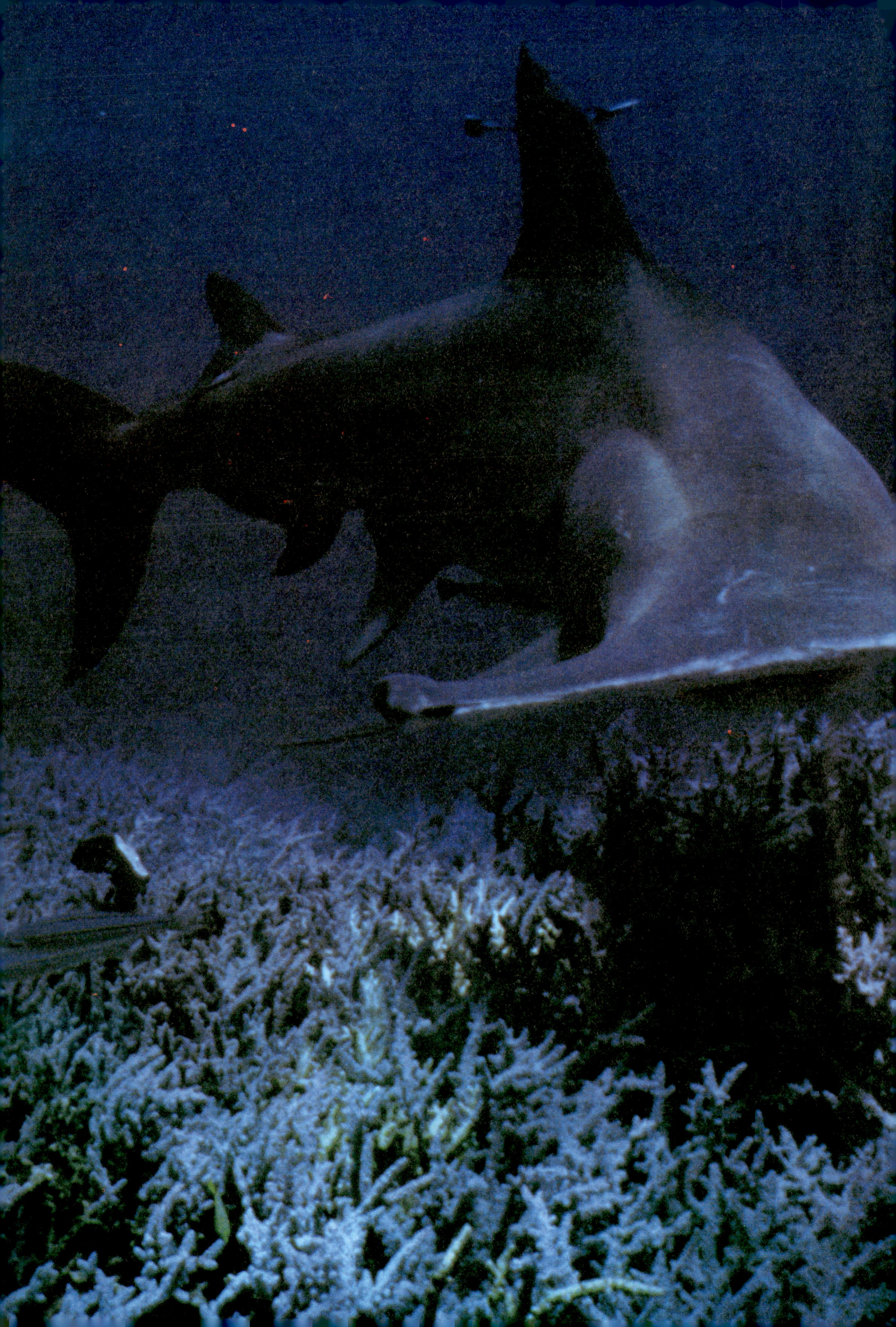

The Hammerhead shark

A catspaw of wind wiped the shine off the smooth sea, painting a purple shadow on the bright, green-blue waters of the Gulf of Mexico. The ruffled surface water sped shorewards while, below, waters from the shallows warmed by a spring sun flowed out to sea. Sometimes at about this time of year, the usual pattern of warm water inshore, cold further out, was reversed and a chill from the deeps crept closer to the shore, while the sun-warmed waters spread out through the cold deeps. There, the warmth brought new life to the plankton, and small fishes in shoals followed the currents.

A long shelf of sand rose gently from the sea floor to the water's edge where it joined the wind-dried buff sands of the beach. The waters rolled into the shore gently and rhythmically while the spring morning shone with promise. Off shore some 200m away floating gulls rose hurriedly into the air and hung there, screaming warnings. A dark fin below them slit the surface of the quiet sea. A dark olive, the fin was soon joined by others. Slowly the fins cut curving patterns through the turning tide, then disappeared beneath the smooth swell.

Seven sleek olive-grey shapes slipped through the shallow water. All were hammerhead sharks. Their bodies sometimes gleamed palely as they banked and turned showing the white of their underparts. They swam slowly in a circle for nearly an hour as the chill currents from the deeps filtered patchily through the warmer waters. Little by little they moved away from the shallow water, following the warmth out to sea.

They read the pattern of temperature changes as these registered along their bodies and tasted the increase in salinity as they headed out to sea. The sharks closely matched each other in size; all were females about three metres long, mature, agile and strong.

A short distance ahead of them a group of largemouth black bass swam lazily, feeding here and there on the small silver fish that were themselves feeding on the plankton. The largest of the bass noticed nothing until a storm of swirling water hit him. He could only have experienced a splintered second of alarm before he died. The bass and two others of his group disappeared whole into the jaws and down to the stomachs of the sharks. Two other bass beat a frantic retreat towards a cluster of rocks on the seabed, one of the large fish passing quite close to a shark but the strangely wide-spaced eyes stared at it without interest.

Near the rocks that now sheltered the remaining bass, a T-shaped head turned slightly to and fro as a small male hammerhead watched the females circling slowly out to sea. He was little more than a metre long and his companions, a short way behind him, were about the same size. The school of females were to the youngster's left as he watched them from around a corner of rock that hid his body from their view. For some minutes his crescent tail, with its long upper caudal, swung slowly to hold him still as the tide flowed past him. The tidal currents brought with them new information. His skin was alive with sensations but it was several minutes before their cause swam into sight. A group of male hammerheads appeared to his right swimming along a chilly strand of water.

The group swam on a course that carried them nearer to the

The bizarrely shaped head of the hammerhead shark makes it easy to recognise, even when swimming underwater. A native of warm subtropical and tropical seas, the hammerhead has a streamlined body and lightweight, cartilaginous skeleton making it a strong, powerful swimmer. It is found in deep water near the sea-bed where it feeds on crabs and barnacles. It also eats small fish, squid, stingrays and even smaller sharks. It is noted for its aggressive nature although attacks on people are rare. However, rogue males sometimes patrol popular beaches and may be attracted by the movement of people swimming offshore in the ocean.

females. There were three males in the approaching group, all about three metres long. As they came closer it was clear that they looked less sleek and well fed than the females. For several days they had eaten very little. Occasionally they had opened their jaws as they passed through a shoal of small fish and swallowed a mouthful of them, but they had turned their great crosspiece heads away from other, more satisfying, prey. Their long bodies had slowly absorbed the fine, nutritious oil stored in their large livers and burned up its latent energy. Now, lighter and thinner, they were ready to mate.

A male hammerhead with a notch in the lower caudal of his tail became agitated, swimming in a half circle. Suddenly he broke from his arc and swam directly towards a female. The youngster watched as the male glided alongside her. She twitched away from him and flashed her teeth at his flank as he hurriedly banked clear. Dipping his broad head to one side, he turned quickly towards a darker female. She continued to swim beside him, showing scant interest in him even when he nudged her with the front edge of his wide head.

He butted her again, quite roughly, and again. They had wandered clear of the female school and the other males were swimming at a respectful distance from the group of females. The notched male persisted, rolling his chosen mate over, carressing her with the abrasive scales that studded his skin. He looped under and over her until his body wound round hers like a stiff scroll. Behind his pelvic fin his claspers were erect but he struggled to make the insertion in vain. The stiffness of his spine seemed to make the position impossible. In his effort to place himself better, he seized her back above her pectoral fins. His teeth scored her skin but did not dig deep. She lay almost still in the water turning her body slightly so that he might move into a better position. His claspers entered her and they mated.

The male slipped away from her and swam alongside her for some minutes before breaking away towards what his nostrils told him was cooler water.

The young male had observed the struggles of the two adults and now left the shelter of his rock, swimming quickly away to join his own companions. They had stayed in the shelter of the nursery waters close to the shore for longer than most hammerheads. Many had left at the same time their mothers had swum to deeper water. These few young males had stayed through the winter but now they turned to the open seas. Some time earlier they had swum out for a couple of kilometres but turned back. Now they swam out for a slightly longer distance and turned towards the north. It was not a steady course they took for they cut away to the east after some three hours. The sea messages picked up through the organs along their bodies drew them further out into the Gulf.

Far out ahead of them the young hammerheads were conscious of a faint but unusually interesting struggle and they found its call

This hammerhead shark struggles fiercely and thrashes its whole body wildly having been caught in a large fishing net. Although sharks account for only one per cent of the total fish caught in the world annually, they are eaten as food, their flesh being lean and tasty. The liver contains oils which are rich in Vitamin A, and sharks were once an important source of this essential nutrient before methods were discovered of manufacturing it commercially in laboratories. In China and the Far East the fins of the soupfin shark are regarded as a great delicacy and are a vital ingredient in the famous sharkfin soup, beloved of oriental cooks. Sharkskin, or shagree, can be polished and dyed to make attractive shoes and garments.

*Opposite page
Like most cartilaginous fish, the hammerhead shark has a typical heterocercal tail of which the top half is longer than the bottom. When swimming, the tail is balanced by the fixed horizontal pectoral fins and the great, flattened snout. Hammerheads have excellent hearing and rely on this sense to home in on sounds deep in the ocean and locate their food. They use their sense of smell rather than their poor eyesight to feed as they see only in black and white and cannot focus well.*

irresistible. They swam more quickly now in an untidy arrowhead formation and as they pushed through the water the sensations grew stronger until their heads were beating with them. By this time they could hear the sounds of a great commotion throbbing through the water. Nearly two kilometres behind the three large males were cutting the surface here and there with their taut dorsal fins on a converging course.

The youngsters reached the scene first by a few minutes. A large shape lay at the surface, wallowing in the gentle swell, and making strange sounds but the young shark's attention was rivetted on the frantic threshings of a great mass of fish close by the large shape. At the surface men were shouting as they tried to free a jammed winch. While they wrestled, their net, bulging with fish, trailed in the sea only metres away.

The small hammerheads barely hesitated before charging the panicking mass in front of them. They bit off parts of fish that protruded from the mesh and severed the strands of the net in their feverish efforts to get at the fish inside. One of the youngsters quickly became entangled in the mesh but, careless of his predicament, continued to snap up the fish within his reach.

The three large males had finished with their pre-mating fast and were slamming through the sea at 40km per hour, their sensors feeding them information about the prey ahead as they made a concentrated drive to reach the prize. They closed in on the scene and pitched into the net, rending it and gulping down the fish inside. The young hammerhead caught in the toils of the net had a glimpse of the open jaws of an adult as the great fish swooped towards him. The teeth-fringed jaws swallowed him up entirely.

The net had so large a hole in it by this time that the fishermen noticed their catch escaping. One caught up a rifle from the bridgehouse and fired at one of the hammerheads as he broke the surface. Three heavy calibre bullets bit home but the shark twisted out of

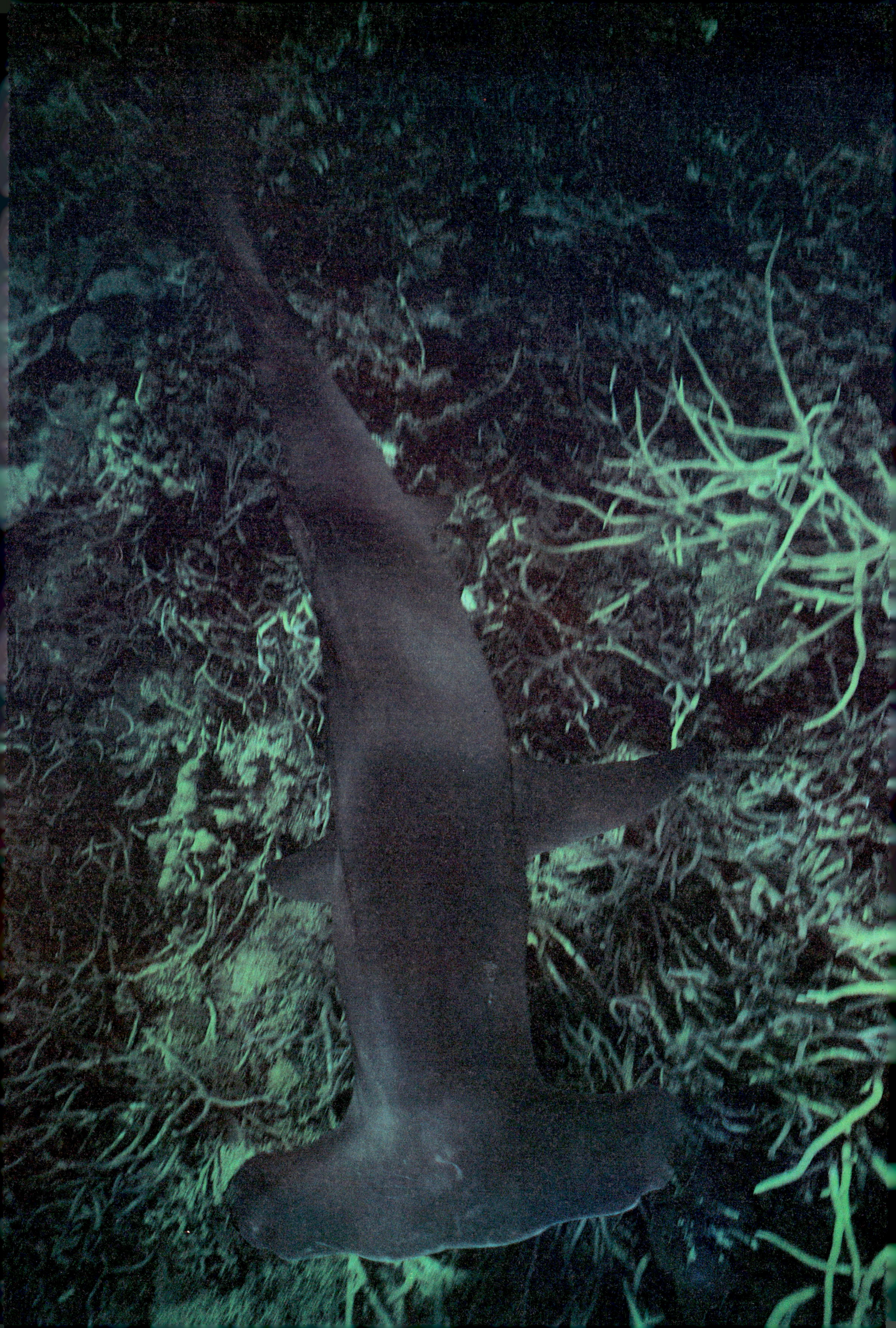

the fisherman's sight, still biting and feeding. The blood from his wounds joined the already clouded water and drew the response of one of his companions. A huge bite behind his dorsal fin made him twist to break clear but he only helped his attacker to sink his teeth in further. The attacking shark shook its head and rotated its body until the mouthful was ripped clear of the wounded shark's back.

The victim had suffered a disabling wound and the other sharks crashed into him, tearing off mouthfuls of flesh and cartilage, but it was not until most of his organs had been consumed that he, himself, stopped tearing at other fish. The sea was a frenzy of foam and blood and still the sharks, even the immature ones that survived, attacked and tore at the catch and at the dead shark.

Two of the young sharks broke away from the carnage, swimming north-east rapidly, but the two surviving large males swam slowly round the broken net and the wreckage of the catch. As the light of day died slowly out of the sky one of the hammerheads swam briskly in towards the boat and butted it hard twice before swimming away to the north, perhaps drawn by the rich waters of the North Carolinas.

The youngsters maintained a steady course for a while. As the moon rose they encountered four more males of their own size and joined the school. They swam near the surface for a few kilometres and the sea around their bodies flickered with phosphorescence. Their shapes looked dark against the greenish light that washed about their bodies. Then they banked, using their great heads to plane to deeper levels on the way to the north. Not until next spring or early summer would they return to the warm waters of the Gulf.

Little is known about the hammerhead shark and the function of its two long, hammerlike lobes. The eyes and nostrils, separated by quite a distance, are located at the ends of the lobes as shown in this photograph. It is thought that the lobes may function as special balancers to compensate for the fact that the shark has no stabilising keels on its tail and its pectoral fins are shortened.

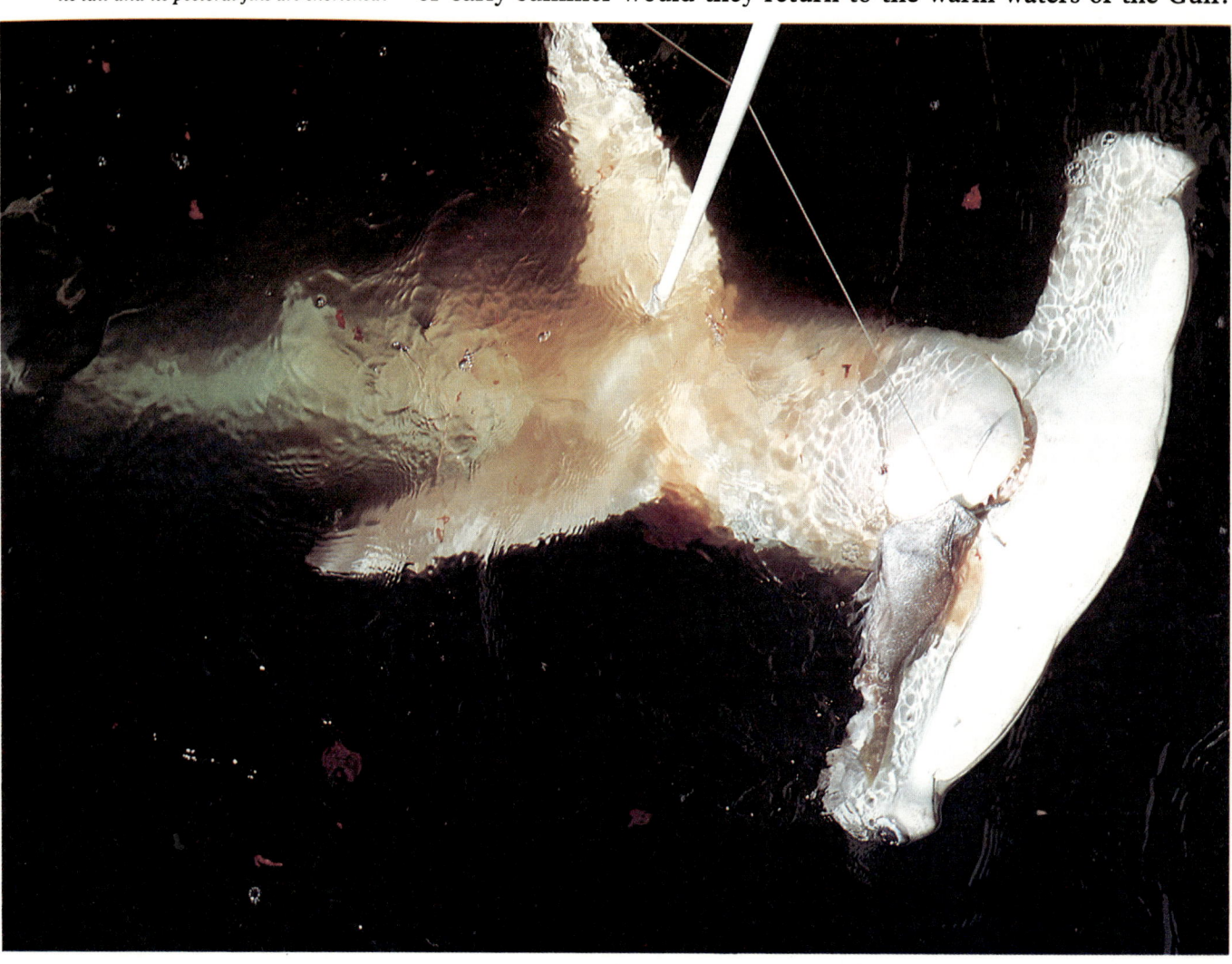

This sand tiger shark, Carcharias taurus, is showing its long, thin teeth. The teeth are arranged in rows in the animal's jaws, the inner row growing outwards to replace the outer teeth as they wear down with constant use. The sand tiger shark is unusual among sharks in so far as it can float weightlessly, using its own intestines when it swallows mouthfuls of air for increased buoyancy.

This shark is snapping at small fish as it swims through the warm waters of the Indian Ocean. Sharks are mainly carnivorous and feed on most fish, crustaceans and invertebrates. However, they are also famed as scavengers and such seemingly inedible objects as boxes, ships' rudders, bottles, tin cans and other refuse have been discovered in the stomachs of dead sharks. Fast-moving hunters, sharks eat as they move, being unable to hang suspended in the water while they feed without sinking. Ironically though, two of the largest members of the shark family, the whale shark and basking shark, are among the least ferocious and feed only on plankton which they filter from the sea-bed by means of special comb-like grill-rakers.

The rogue of the seas

The shark has a formidable reputation as a ferocious predator, which matches that of the most feared four-footed land animal, the tiger. However, unlike the great cat, the shark has few human admirers. It is surprising that its mastery of the seas and the perfection of its form have not won more people to care about its conservation. The shark in all its forms is truly remarkable. Not many sea creatures match its sensory acuteness and the force of its attack. The beautifully hydrodynamic lines of its body and its cartilaginous skeleton have remained barely touched by the millions of years that witnessed the evolution of other fish. It would be wrong to consider the shark as a lingering relic of the Devonian era or a species, like the coelacanth, left behind by a quirk of evolution. The shark achieved a form that the passage of time has proved to be suitable to its lifestyle, so its body has made few adjustments for some millions of years.

Sharks of between 250 and 350 species inhabit the world's oceans. Their forms range from the Australian wobbegong (*Orectolobus maculatus*), a flattened species with a dorsal fin which is elongated to meet its tail, to the saw sharks (of the family *Pristiophoridae*) and the bottom-dwelling lantern shark (*Etmopterus spinax*), whose skin is equipped with small light organs, which help it to survive in the black depths of 2,000 metres.

The **great hammerhead** (*Sphyrna mokarran*, once known as *S. tudes*), is the largest of the family. The great hammerheads frequently grow to 4.60m, and the longest ever measured was 5.58m. They inhabit tropical waters, and few will be found in areas cooler than 23°C so they rarely migrate further north than the equator. The great hammerheads' teeth have serrated edges, and their pectoral fins have a distinctive sickle shape.

The **common hammerhead** (*S. zygaena*: see *At a glance* panel) ranges north to the 45th parallel, although it is uncommon so far north. The lower temperature limit of the waters that it favours is about 18°C. The common hammerhead has smooth-edged teeth, with only a few showing slight serrations. The leading edge of its head is straighter and shows less of the scalloping found in any other species.

The white-tipped reef shark, commonly found around tropical reefs.

S. lewini (once known as *S. diplana*) grows to about 3.65m and lives in much the same areas as the great hammerhead. Its head, similar to that of *S. mokarran*, has a marked, scallop-shaped indentation in the centre of its leading edge, and its teeth are smooth-edged.

S. couardi, another large hammerhead, grows to about the same size as the common hammerhead but has white tips to its pectoral fins. It inhabits West African waters.

S. tudes (before revision, *S. mokarran*) is one of the three species of small hammerheads. It grows to about 1.50m in length, and lives in localised areas in the western Mediterranean, and in the Gulf of Mexico to as far south as Uruguay.

S. media, another of the small species, swims the coastal Pacific waters from northern lower California to Panama, and from Panama down the coast of Chile in the eastern Pacific.

S. corona has a more localised range than any other hammerhead. It inhabits inshore waters of the eastern Pacific from southern Mexico to Colombia. This species grows to about 1.50m.

The **bonnet shark** (*S. tiburo*) is sometimes called the shovelhead. It has the roundest head of all the hammerheads. Unlike other hammerheads, the bonnet shark's outer four or five teeth in its lower jaw have no defined cutting edge and no cusps. There are two subspecies of bonnet shark: *S. t.tiburo* inhabits waters from southern Brazil to New England; and *S. t.vespertina* lives in Pacific waters from Ecuador to southern California. Both subspecies prefer inshore waters. They are grey or a greyish brown above, shading gradually to a pale grey on their undersides. Few grow to more than 1.50m long but a few achieve 1.80m. It is not as active a fish as most other hammerheads, and is not known to attack man.

S. blochii, another of the small hammerheads, has the widest head of all the family. Its head is also the shortest, measured from back to front. The width of the head is half the length of the fish's body. It is also unusual among hammerheads for the position of its nostrils, which occur halfway between the outer edges of the head and the centre point. All other hammerheads have nostrils on the outer edges of their heads. **S. blochii** are inhabitants of the Indo-Pacific.

Different members of the hammerhead family, or Sphyrna, *have varying head shapes, ranging from the hammerlike projections of* S. blochii *on which the eyes and nostrils are widely spaced to much smaller extensions on other sharks.*

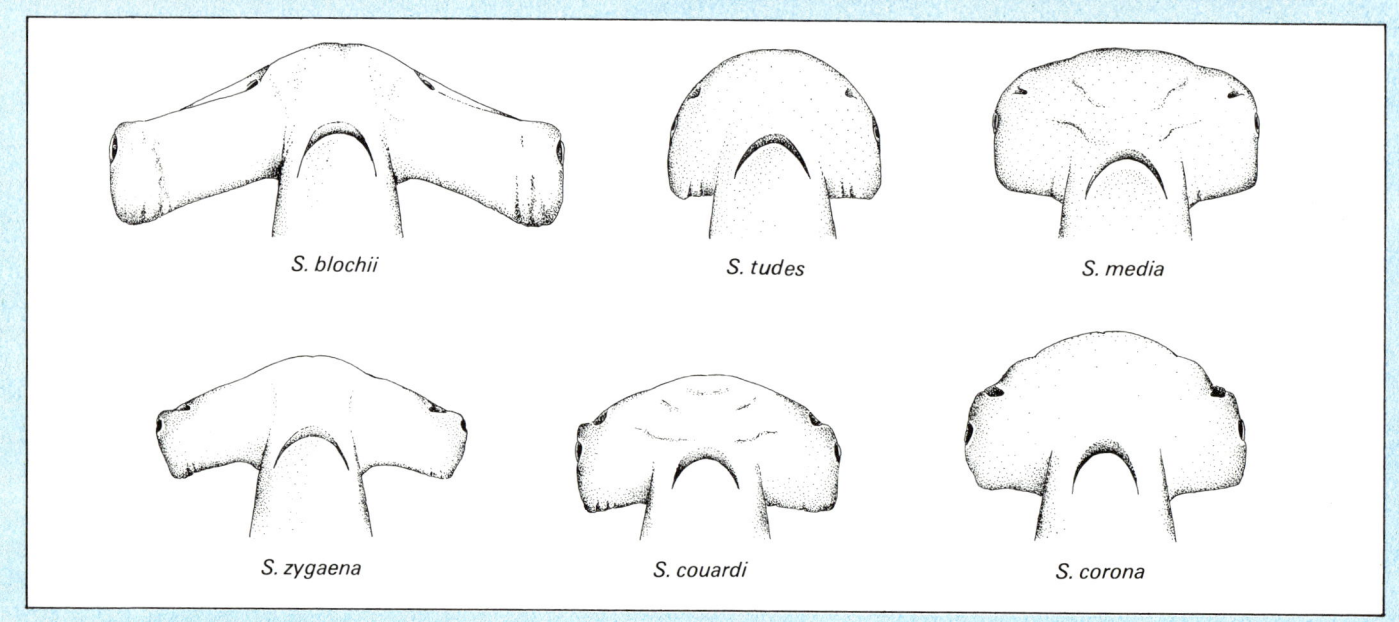

S. blochii

S. tudes

S. media

S. zygaena

S. couardi

S. corona

Thresher shark

Blue shark

Leopard shark

Hammerhead shark

Great white shark

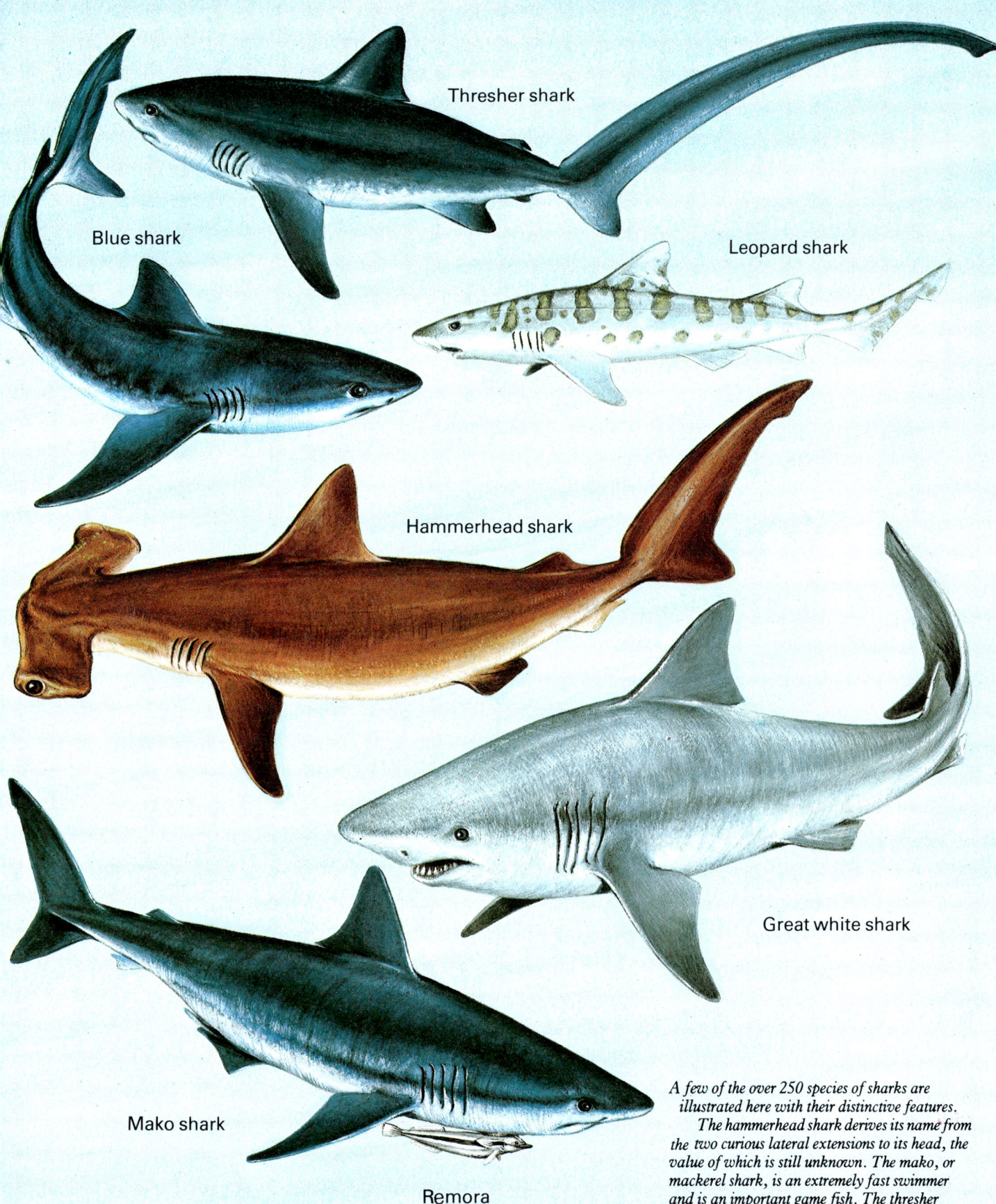

Mako shark

Remora

Fellow travellers
Sharks, despite their reputation for savagery, frequently find themselves in company that shows no signs of fearing them. Two main types of fish swim in association with sharks, pilot fish and remoras. Neither kind is a parasite nor do they live symbiotically, serving the shark. They are commensals, feeding on the same foods as their large and predatory companion.

Pilot fish are often seen swimming ahead of a shark, so early observers concluded that they were guiding the shark into a position where the hunter could see its prey — an idea discounted now that more is known of the shark's excellent sensory system. More than one kind of fish lives in this way with sharks. Three of the commonest are the rainbow runner (*Elagatis bipinnulates*), *Seriola zonata* and starry Jack (*Caranx stellatus*).

A few of the over 250 species of sharks are illustrated here with their distinctive features.
The hammerhead shark derives its name from the two curious lateral extensions to its head, the value of which is still unknown. The mako, or mackerel shark, is an extremely fast swimmer and is an important game fish. The thresher shark uses the huge upper lobe of its tail fin to thresh the water and concentrate shoals of fish before charging into the middle and seizing its victims. The leopard shark, a native of the Pacific coast of North America, swims constantly, day and night, or it would sink. The blue shark lives in the open seas and will attack small fish, other sharks and even man. A fierce predatory shark, the great white patrols the coastline of Australia and may reach up to 12m in length and weigh in excess of three tonnes.

A fish with a difference
It has been said that a frog and a man are closer to one another biologically than are a shark and a herring. On the face of it, that is a surprising statement, but the shark has several fundamental characteristics that are unfishlike. Whereas a herring's skeleton is composed of many bones, the shark has none. The shark has skin covered with scales which are in effect small, modified teeth unlike the herring's cycloid scales which are flat, bony plates, and the swim bladder a fish uses to control the depth at which it swims is missing in the shark.

The shark's skeleton consists not of bones but of tough, flexible cartilage. For a long time, biologists considered that this was a primitive form of skeleton but, recently, new evidence from the fossil record has led them to conclude that sharks are descended from ancestors that had bony skeletons and that the modern shark's skeleton is a regression to softer tissue. The fish's backbone is partly calcified (though nowhere is it true bone) and provides an ideal anchor against which the powerful swimming muscles of the trunk can act. The shark does not have the developed ribcage found in most fishes, but vestiges of ribs appear as small projections from its backbone. A further difference between sharks and bony fishes lies in the structure of their heads. Fishes such as herring have skulls that are made up of several plates of bone sutured firmly together. The shark's skull consists of a complete block of cartilage, shaped round the brain, auditory and olfactory chambers, and pierced with passages for nerves and vessels.

The shape of the shark is beautifully adapted for swimming at bursts of speed. It swims with its dorsal fins erect; in fact, it cannot fold them down. The fish drives itself through the water with an oar-like waving motion of its body, beginning somewhere above the pectoral fins and ending with a broad sweep of the long caudals of the tail. The crescent shape of the upper caudal is ideal to give speed. Its action does tend to drive the shark slightly downwards though, and this tendency is countered by the constantly spread pectoral fins which give the fish 'lift'. The pectoral fins, acting as planes, compensate in part for the shark's lack of a swim bladder, so long as the fish is moving forwards. The shark is so well adapted to its swimming function that it requires only a sixth of the power output per kilogramme that would be needed by a submarine of the same weight.

Sharks are sprinters rather than long-distance pursuers. The fastest of them is probably the mackerel (or mako) shark. A small one, about 60cm long, clocked 69km/h in short bursts, and a larger mackerel shark would be able to achieve rather higher speeds. The driving force behind these speeds lies in the shark's muscles, which are of two types, red and white. The red muscle oxides fat to create energy, a system that is about twice as efficient as using carbohydrates or protein. Myoglobin is the substance that transports the essential oxygen into the red muscle fibres, which are well supplied with blood. The shark uses the red muscle tissue when cruising, and the greater bulk of the white fibres for sprints. These fibres function without using molecular oxygen but break down glycogen to produce energy. Sharks, being ocean cruisers, have a larger preponderance of red muscle fibres than most other fish.

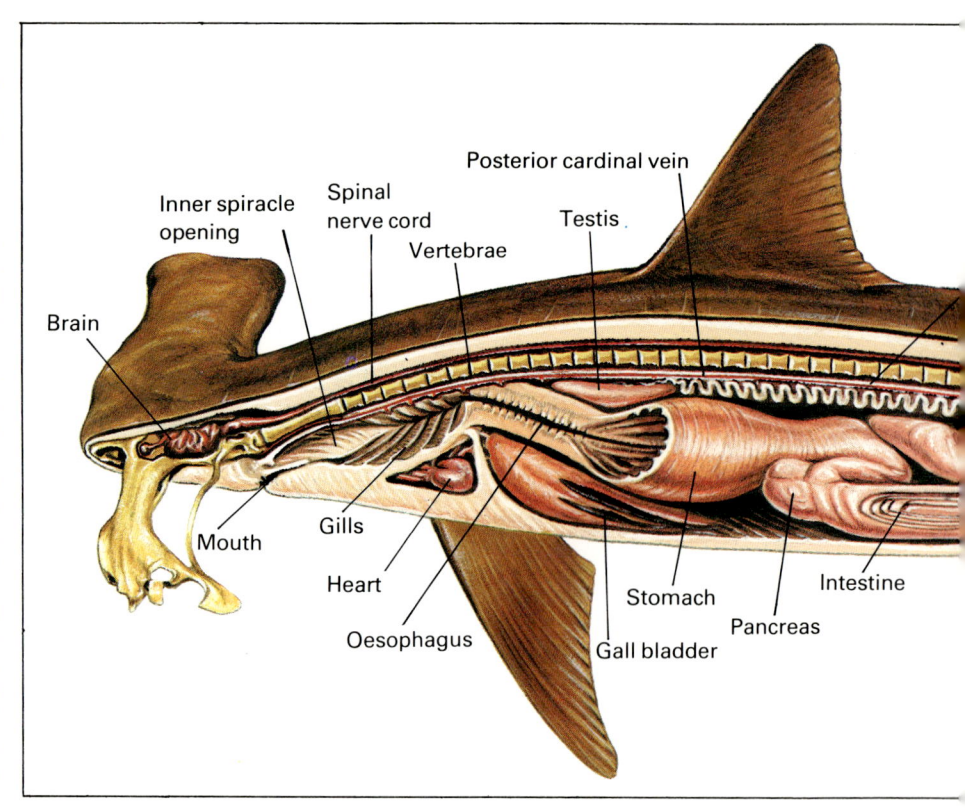

The shark must swim or it must sink to the ocean floor, which it may do sometimes. Its buoyancy is increased, in the absence of a swim bladder filled with gas, by a store of oil in its liver. The two lobes of a shark's liver sometimes fill the entire body cavity of the fish; and as much as 80 per cent, but more usually half of the liver, may be oil. Most of the shark's energy reserves are concentrated in this reservoir enabling it to swim for long periods with little or no food. A female hammerhead may have a liver of 30kg for a body length of 3.70m. Its proportion in relation to the body as a whole may vary greatly: hammerheads of 4-4.50m measured in July had livers of 15-20kg, and of 40-50kg in October when seasonal mating and bearing young were over.

Sharks have a U-shaped digestive tract, the arms of which are unequal in length. Food is swallowed whole down the oesophagus and stored temporarily in the cardiac stomach. It continues round a 180° bend into the pyloric stomach where it is digested more fully. The pyloris leads to a short duodenum and on to the intestine, which has a spiral valve with the advantage of offering a large absorption area for its fairly short length. The food waste passes through the rectum and the cloaca as it leaves the body.

Shark sense
Man is a visual animal; although he can touch, smell, taste and hear, he depends most of all on sight to make his way in the world. This leaves him at a disadvantage when he tries to imagine what it might be like to be a shark. The shark's senses perceive a world that is quite different to anything experienced by man, even by a blind man. The shark swims in an environment that reveals itself through

	At a glance Hammerhead shark *Sphyrna zygaena*
Class	Chondrichthyes
Subclass	Elasmobranchii
Family	Sphyrnidae
Length	3-4.5m. The females appear to grow a little larger than the males.
Length of snout	78.8cm
Weight	412kg
Method of reproduction	Internal fertilisation.
Development	Oviparous. One family may give birth to as many as 37 young in a season.
Colour	Dark olive or brownish-grey along the back, paling to near-white under the belly. The tips of the fins are dark, often black.
Diet	Fish, including Spanish mackerel, other sharks, herring, bass, skate, sting-rays, barnacles, crabs and squid.

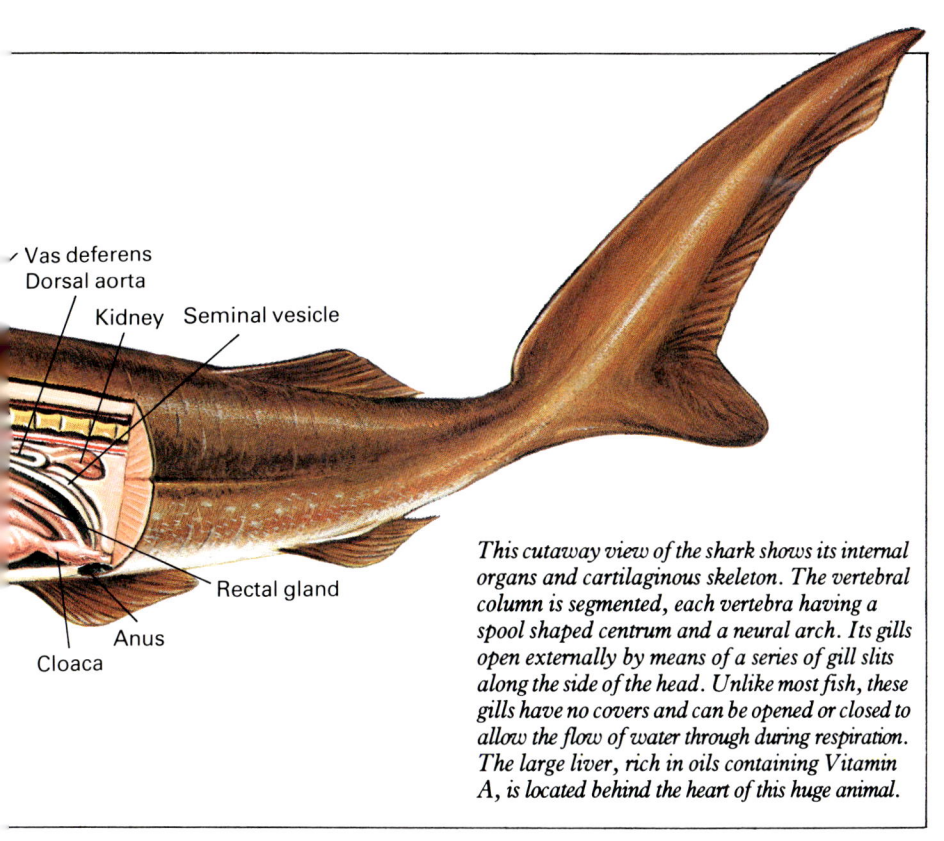

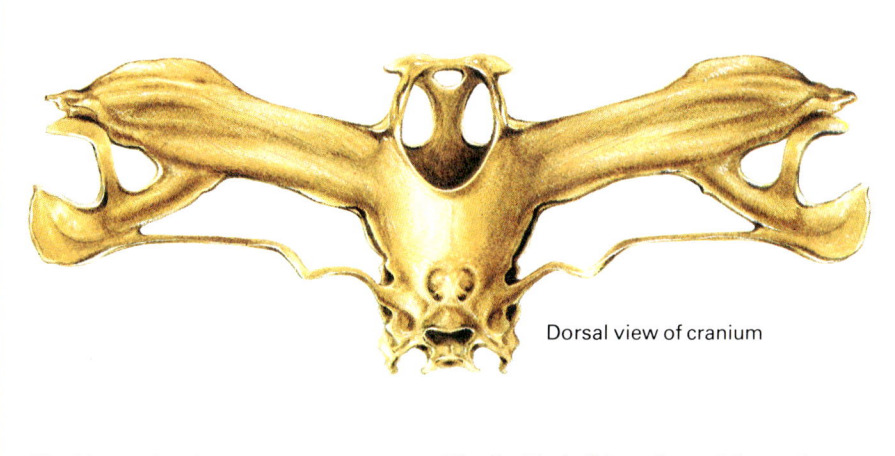

This cutaway view of the shark shows its internal organs and cartilaginous skeleton. The vertebral column is segmented, each vertebra having a spool shaped centrum and a neural arch. Its gills open externally by means of a series of gill slits along the side of the head. Unlike most fish, these gills have no covers and can be opened or closed to allow the flow of water through during respiration. The large liver, rich in oils containing Vitamin A, is located behind the heart of this huge animal.

The shark's skull is made up of the cranium, which houses the brain; paired capsules for the hearing, sight and olfactory organs; and the jaws. Unlike those of a mammal, the teeth are not fitted into a socket and grow from the tooth-bed. Behind each active row of teeth on the perimeter of the shark's mouth there lie five or six rows of reserve teeth. The active teeth are replaced about once every eight days. The eyes are covered by a nictitating membrane when the shark is approached by a strange object. However, it is present only in the more highly evolved sharks.

The shark's skin is covered with small placoid scales, a form of modified teeth. Each scale is made up of dentine, with a pulp cavity, and is covered with a layer of enamel. Their purpose is uncertain and they offer little in the way of armoured protection. They may hold a layer of non-turbulent water close to the body and so decrease drag and increase laminar flow. Also, they may create small vortices as they pass through the water, thus aiding the shark's swimming movements. Although the shark's lateral sensory organs may provide the fish with information on the state of the vortices, the significance of the scales is still not fully understood.

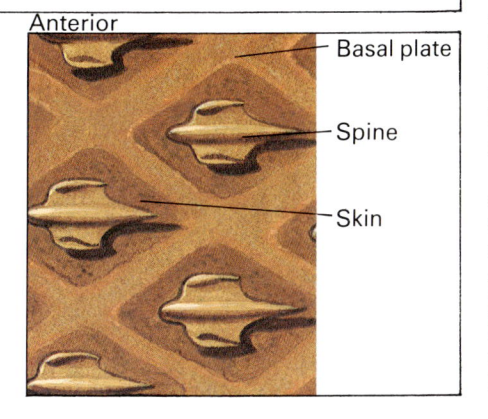

minute alterations in pressure and fine changes in the taste and smell of surrounding water, sounds and sight, probably in that order.

Like most fish, sharks have lines of sensors along the sides of their bodies. These lateral lines warn the shark of any movements in its environment. This complex of sensors consists of canals of fluid in the shark's head and along both sides of its body. They run beneath the skin and connect with the skin's surface through tubes. Extensions of the shark's nervous system, in the form of hair-like processes called neuromasts, protrude into the canals. When the water pressure is even faintly disturbed, the fluid in the canals moves, vibrating the neuromasts, which stimulates an impulse to flash along the shark's nerves to its brain. The lateral canals are easily seen, but there are many others beneath the fish's skin that are invisible to an observer. These sensors may detect low frequency vibrations, such as those made by a struggling fish. Higher frequency vibrations are probably heard.

On the front of the head, pore-like openings, called ampullae of Lorenzini, are believed to respond to the electrical impulses that radiate from prey making intense muscular efforts. These senses also respond to the salinity of the surrounding water, its pressure changes and temperature.

Between the scales on the shark's skin are sensory pits. They lie along the fish's back, flanks and around the lower jaw. They resemble taste buds but they may operate differently, perhaps responding to pressure as well as chemical changes in the water.

The shark's organs of smell account for its reputation as a 'swimming nose'. Two-thirds of its brain's weight account for its smelling apparatus. The nostrils of a hammerhead open on the front edge of its head. Each nostril leads to a sac consisting of folds of tissue, increasing the surface over which the water flows and making the olfactory sac more sensitive. A flap which can cover the nostrils divides the inflowing water from the outflow.

With this array of excellent senses, the shark might not regret the lack of first-class vision. In fact, the shark's sight is better than zoologists assumed up to recently. Most species of shark have no cones in their retina, but they are well supplied with rods so, although they lack colour perception, their awareness of light is good. The retina is backed by a *tapetum lucidum*, which is a series of plates covered with guanine crystals to make a reflecting surface which directs light back through the eye to intensify the light image. The shark's eyes in most respects are like those of most other vertebrates. Its eyes are not, however, protected by their eyelids, which are not moveable. A nictitating membrane slides across from the side to clean and protect each eye, but this does not include the light, so the shark can see at all times. The hammerhead will cover its eyes with the nictitating membrane when approaching a prey.

Sharks have good directional hearing, especially in the low frequency range. A struggling fish makes noises below the 100 cycles-per-second range, and it is in this sound area that sharks hear best. A lemon shark's hearing was measured and found to be sensitive between 640-10 cycles per second. This compares with a human hearing range of 20,000-20 cycles per second.

The Pelican

A milky white mist rolled softly over the invisible reed beds, the morning sun touching the opaque screen with pewter light. Above the mist bank, the sky was a distant pallid blue, threatening a day of unusual heat. Islands of tall reed tops and clumps of willow pierced the barely undulating blanket. High above, a diagonal flight of pelicans looked down on the white moisture that hid their homes from sight.

The precise sequence of their flight held a grace that would have escaped a man-made formation. The soft rise and fall rhythm of their great wings, beating once each second and all instinctively together, made the line seem to pulse with an unhurried energy of its own. Each bird, except the leader, flew with economy using the turbulent air left by the bird in front. Their flight was to be a long one – over 100km – to the fishing ground. Whenever a thermal (see page 91) rose near their path, the pelicans glided as the warm air wafted them high to allow a long shallow dive to the next thermal or to the resumption of slow, flapping flight.

The leader drew back to a position further along the procession, letting another pelican do the harder work at the front. The move left the rhythm unimpaired, and the pelicans, heads gently cushioned back on their curving necks, flew on to the oxbow lake hidden under a patch of mist.

The sparkles of rippled water penetrated the thinning mist as the pelicans made a shallow glide towards their fishing ground. They wheeled slightly to turn into the wind, skimmed low over the bright water, backed their great wings and dropped their pink feet into their second element.

Nine weeks earlier, the crude nests had been completed at the delta from which they had flown that morning. The males had finished the struggles to and fro, bearing grass and small sticks in

The young pelican chicks are born naked, pink and helpless but within three days they grow a dark brown, downy coat which gradually lightens in colour. At first they feed on liquid food which their parents dribble down their bills, but later their diet changes to one of regurgitated fish. The chicks, in their enthusiasm to eat, sometimes thrust their heads deep into a parent's bill and gullet to obtain the food. They learn to feed by pecking at a red spot on the adult's bill and this gave rise to the old belief that the young were fed on the mother's blood, and to the heraldic notion of piety. After about three weeks the chicks learn to walk and congregate together in groups known as 'pods'. They soon learn to fish, if living by the water, and start flying at 60-70 days.

their bills to lay them before their chosen females, who then piled them into a nest, cementing the materials into a solid mass with mud and their own droppings. The eggs had been laid, patiently incubated by both parent birds, and most had hatched out their chicks successfully. The helpless chicks had lolled their naked bodies among the shards of broken eggshells, utterly helpless for nearly a week. They were even incapable of raising their heads from the ground for much of that time. Anxious parents dribbled a liquid mess of half-digested fish into their offsprings' mouths.

The chicks had soon begun a period of rapacious obsession with feeding. Their lives revolved round the attentions of their hard-worked parents. There was no question of dribbling food into the bills of supine chicks then. The young birds, covered with a dark brown down after a fortnight of life, banged at the bills of the adult birds, demanding access to the contents. When the great bills opened, the chicks used the adults' pouches as feeding troughs, plunging their heads and shoulders inside to gobble up the half-eaten fish inside.

The pelicans had flown to the oxbow lake in search of more food for the demanding crèche in the colony at the marshy river mouth. In another month, many of the chicks would be sprouting feathers and swimming short distances from the nests to fish for their own food. They would still demand food from the weary parents, but a fortnight or so later the young fledgelings would attempt their first flights, staggering into the air, their plump bodies heavier than those of their parents.

In the meantime, the parent birds searched far away from the colony for food to sustain their broods. The morning mist had fled, and the day was bright with hard light. On the water, the pelicans swam slowly, about 150m offshore. Their heads were tucked comfortably on to their necks, the plumage of their heads and necks flushed with the pink of the breeding season. Most of the birds shone a clear white, but there were two that were still speckled with the brown of their immature plumage.

The water's surface danced with life as it warmed in the sun. Small insects skittered across the gently lapping lake. The ponderous yellow bills swung here and there as the pelicans' orange irises peered into the water. An observer might have detected a pattern of movement at about five hours after dawn. The pelicans had had little success in their fishing, and now, lying high in the water, they slowly cruised into a line that lay roughly parallel with a shallow beach.

The line curled forward slightly at each end, and the 18 pelicans began to thresh at the water with their wings. They beat the surface with their huge beaks until their line of advance was a curve of white foaming water. The water between the beaters and the shore was flecked now and then with rings as fish leapt to the surface in panic. Soon, the extremities of the arc of pelicans nearly touched the shore. The water in between was alive with small fish that desperately tried to escape the violent upheaval to their rear, but there was no way forward. The pelicans swept their pouched beaks into the water to scoop them up in mouthfuls.

The extended pouches filled like fishing nets to trap the fish. Then the pelicans raised their heads to swallow their prey whole. Mouthful after mouthful they scooped and swallowed, their straining pouches distended with more than 13 litres of water and struggling fish. When they could swallow no more, they paddled slowly up the muddy beach. They lurched and limped onto dry land. Their gait was almost ridiculously clumsy after the grace of their flight and the impressiveness of their display on the water. One of the immature pelicans and an older female toppled sideways to lay threshing with their wings for nearly a minute before they could find their feet

These great white pelicans (Pelecanus onocrotalus) *are very gregarious birds and flock together in large numbers beside lakes. They usually nest in such colonies, and in the breeding season the males develop a rosy hue to their plumage. They breed on the ground, the males collecting the nesting material and carrying it in their bills to the females. Two or three elongated white eggs are laid and both male and female birds take their turns at incubating them over the 35-37 day incubation period. The pelicans return to their traditional nesting sites every year, many of which are centuries old. Most nesting sites are inaccessible, except by air, to avoid predators and human interference, and thus pelicans may even nest on the summit of a huge rock.*

85

again. The weight of food in their gullets and pouches made their normal clumsiness on land still more precarious.

It was nearly an hour before the birds recovered from the orgy of feeding. Finally they roused themselves sufficiently to stretch out their wings to dry. With slow flaps, they loosened the sodden strands of feathers so that the hot sun could do its work of drying out. The pelicans' feathers are less water resistant than those of many other water birds. They preened the drying plumage, stroking the secretions of their preening glands, situated near their tails, into the bedraggled feathers.

The sun had passed its zenith before the birds felt able to make the return journey to the colony comfortably. In the meantime, several pelicans had taken other fish from the far side of the lake. All the pelicans entered the water again. They swam into the wind and, one after another, 'wound up' for take-off. The long wings stretched out and, the tips flicking the water for a few strokes, the birds launched themselves into the air with little effort. They circled the lake until all their number had joined the flight and set course for the marshlands of the great river's estuary.

The afternoon sun slanted across the reed beds of the colony when the flight of pelicans circled into the wind to make their landing. A pod of about 80 chicks jostled together on a raft of matted reeds, desperately eager for food. Parent birds waddled up to them and sorted out which chicks were their own. With gulping convulsions of their necks, they regurgitated the glutinous contents of their gullets while the chicks battered at their beaks and breasts for attention. As soon as the bills opened, the young birds struggled to get inside, so great was their greed.

These pelicans are taking off with a great flapping of wings from Lake Nakuru in Kenya. Although they are superb fliers and well adapted to swimming in order to catch their food, they are remarkably clumsy, ungainly birds on land. They can sustain soaring flight for long distances and may cover hundreds of kilometres when they migrate south in the winter. They often fly in large flocks, taking off on the thermal updraughts of wind and rising spirally on the rising air currents until they reach their desired height and fly in a large 'V' shaped formation. Their bodies are highly specialised for flight, being permeated throughout with air spaces.

On the edge of one of the reed beds, a male pelican approached his mate, still sitting on her eggs which were laid late in the season. He staggered onto the lumpy ground and began to thread his way between the other nests that crowded the spot. Other pelicans pecked at him as he brushed past them. When he came near to his mate, he raised his bill until it was nearly vertical. The female bird responded by shuffling backwards from the nest, raising her bill in greeting, and giving a little bow. Her eggs were almost ready to hatch, but there was small chance that the young would be fully fledged in time to join the migration flights in the autumn. The female pelican waddled through the crowded nests to the water's edge, rousing another female, to make an annoyed braying sound. The pelicans rarely made sounds, although the chicks squeaked for attention.

As the female entered the water, a blanket of silence lay over the promontory of reeds she had just left. A pair of large crows flapped low above the reeds. The adult pelicans watched, some of them moving protectively towards their young. At the edge of the floating mat of reeds was a pelican chick, younger than most of the others. It had not done well in the competition for food. Its sibling had pushed it aside often, and taken the greater share. The chick was a poor specimen as it struggled to join the rest of the pod of chicks and the protection of the adults.

The crows spotted its erratic movements as it staggered and slipped over the tangled reeds. They swooped in and landed beside it. It died quickly, and the crows feasted on it until a large male pelican swam towards them and a female pushed through the crowd of youngsters to hiss at and threaten the predators. The crows flew along the edges of the colony on the look-out for more weaklings.

Only the strong pelicans would survive the first year of their lives. Once the first great step was taken and they grew big enough and strong enough to fly, they would moult and their bodies would be prepared for their first migration. It would be about three winter migrations later before they would be mature enough to mate and produce their own broods.

White pelicans sometimes perch on mangrove clumps as in this swamp in the Gambia. Pelicans often live near water and their long, flat bills are adapted to fishing with an elastic, expandible pouch attached to the lower mandible for scooping up fish from the water. It functions in the same way as a fishing net, expanding underwater and filling up with fish as the pelican raises it. Great white pelicans often fish together in a horseshoe formation of eight to 12 birds to create a shadow effect in the water which attracts and bemuses the fish. As they move through the water, they beat their wings and dip their bills in unison to drive the fish into the centre of their formation.

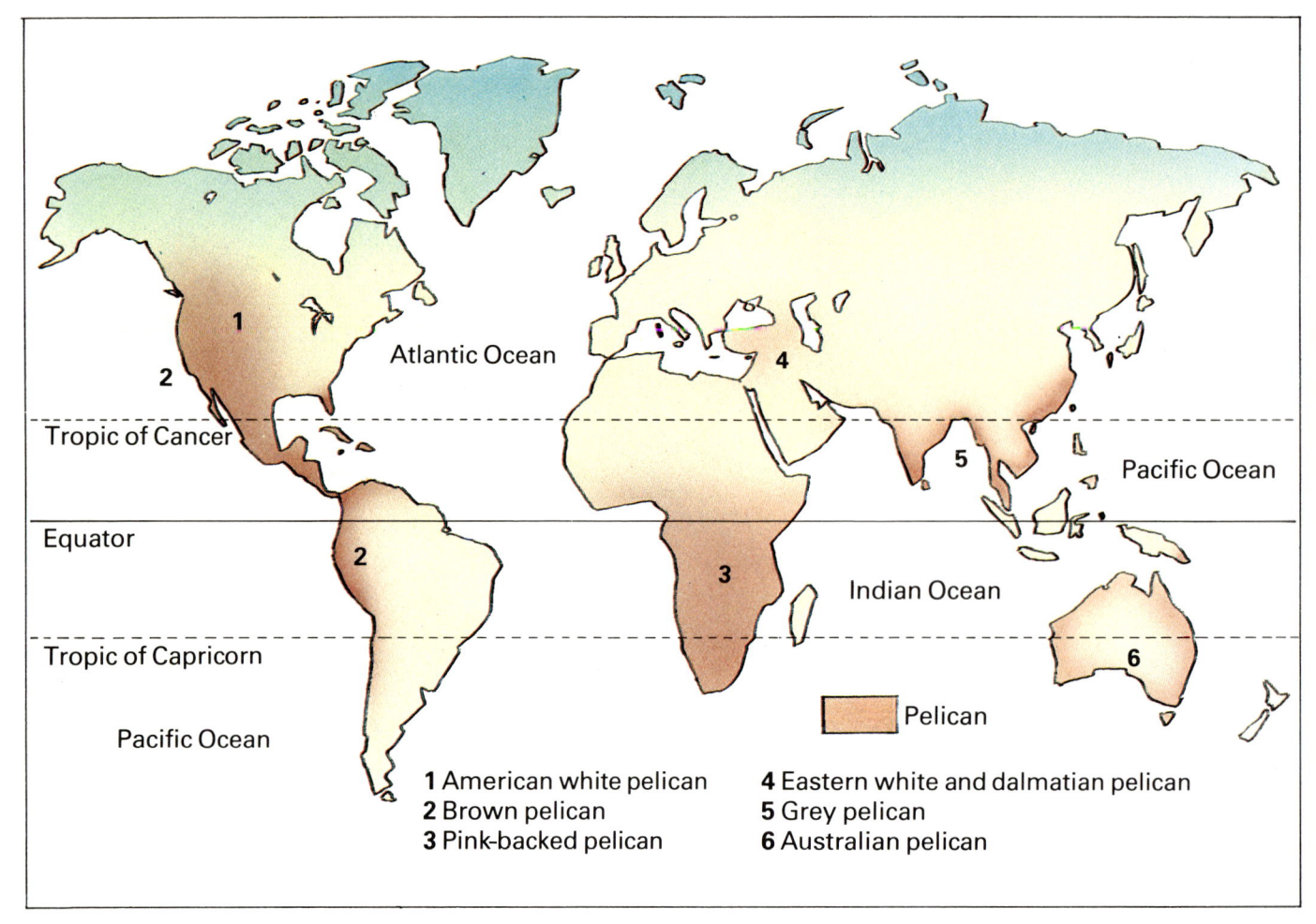

1 American white pelican
2 Brown pelican
3 Pink-backed pelican
4 Eastern white and dalmatian pelican
5 Grey pelican
6 Australian pelican

Pelicans across the world

Pelicans are among the heaviest and bulkiest flying birds in the world. Their grotesque clumsiness on the ground vanishes as soon as they become airborne.

The order of Pelecaniformes includes other expert fishing birds, such as the gannet, the shag, the cormorant family and also those outstanding air pirates, the frigatebirds. There are seven living species of pelicans, all of which live by their skills as fishers. One species, the brown pelican, regularly dives for its prey.

There is cause for concern over the falling numbers of the world's pelicans. As marshes are drained, humans encroach on wild animal habitats, and as the lakes of Central Asia shrink, the areas that pelicans find suitable for breeding diminish. A century ago, the Danube delta provided a home for about 300,000 Dalmatian pelicans while they bred their chicks. Between 1925 and 1935, major onslaughts by men on the breeding birds reduced the numbers drastically. By 1959, only 2,000 Dalmatian pelicans visited this major breeding ground. Now they are protected by law, but parent birds are shot by illegal hunters still while their nests are destroyed by fire and their eggs stolen or broken by fishermen who see the birds as a threat to their own livelihood.

The **eastern white pelican** (*Pelecanus onocrotalus*) is sometimes called the great white pelican. See *At a glance* panel.

The **Dalmatian pelican** (*P. crispus*) is one of only two species seen in Europe, the other being the eastern white pelican. The Dalmatian pelican is rather larger than the white, measuring about 166-185cm from bill to tail. It nests in smaller colonies than the white pelican but is sometimes observed in association with them. The Dalmatian pelican's fishing habits are similar to those of the white species, but it will quite frequently fish alone and will venture fairly well out to sea to fish with other seabirds, such as cormorants.

The Dalmatian pelican has a silvery tinge to its plumage and a crest of curly feathers. Its feet are a leaden grey, and the pouch is a fine clear orange. The primary feathers are black and the secondaries are dark grey.

Females lay between two and four eggs in a clutch and, in Europe, incubation starts in April or May and lasts for up to 40 days. Like all pelicans, the young are born naked and blind, but after a week the young hatchlings can swim. Their plumage is complete after about two and a half months, and the birds can fly away.

The **pink-backed pelican** (*P. rufescens*) is similar to, but smaller than, the white pelican. In the mating season its back is suffused with a beautiful shade of pink. The pink-backed pelican lives in tropical Africa, where it inhabits marshes and lakes south of latitude 16° north.

The **Australian pelican** (*P. conspicillatus*) grows nearly as large as the white pelican. It has a large area of naked skin surrounding the eyes and plumage of a soft grey on the neck. Its wing feathers are mainly black. It is one of the most handsome of the pelican family. The Australian pelican is found throughout areas where there is water in Australia, southern New Guinea and Tasmania.

The **grey pelican** (*P. philippensis*) is the colour its name suggests, paling to a nearly white shade under its belly and with black flight feathers. Its feet are dark brown, and its bill is of pinkish yellow, marked with blue-black spots on the upper part of the beak. Grey pelicans are found from India to southern China, Java and the Philippines.

The **American white pelican** (*P. erythrorhynchus*) is occasionally described as the rough-billed pelican. Its white plumage is marked with a yellow patch on the breast and the wing coverts. It has a yellow-orange bill, and its legs and feet are pink. A disc-like projection appears on its culmen (the upper mandible of its bill) during the breeding season but recedes when the season passes. The American white pelican is found throughout suitably water-rich areas of the western United States, Florida and Central America.

The **brown pelican** (*P. occidentalis*) is the only pelican that dives for food. It tucks back its wings and freefalls from heights of up to 15m to scoop up its prey with great accuracy. As its name suggests, the brown pelican's plumage is a dusky colour which darkens to a chocolate brown in the breeding season. The bird weighs about 3.5kg and has a wingspan of up to 2.30m. It may nest in trees or make shallow scrapes on guano islands.

Like all pelicans, the brown species is a sociable bird, but chicks that clamour to be fed and pester adults which are not their parents are likely to be snapped up and eaten themselves — a fact that runs counter to the pelican's mythical reputation for self-sacrifice. There are six subspecies of brown pelican.

Pink-backed pelican

Brown pelicans

Pelicans are found throughout the world in Africa, Australia, Asia, south-eastern Europe and the Americas. The brown pelican is the only species that dives from a great height into the water to catch fish. The American white pelican has a strange growth on its long bill, whereas the great eastern white has a swollen forehead. The Dalmatian and Australian species breed in large colonies and nest on the ground. The brown and pink backed pelicans, however, perch, roost and nest in trees in smaller colonies of birds.

American white

Great eastern white

Dalmatian

Australian pelican

Grey pelican

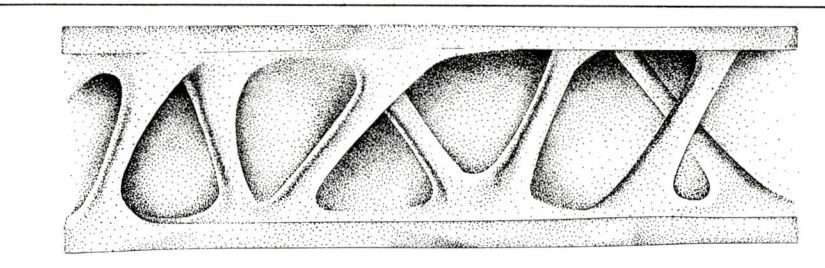

The great white pelican, Pelecanus onocrotalus, has short, sturdy legs and white plumage fading to pale grey. Its feet are webbed to assist swimming and the bill, with its extendible pouch, is long and straight. A subspecies of the great (or eastern) white pelican is the white roseate pelican of eastern and southern Africa. It derives its name from its pink flushed plumage and has a shorter bill than the great white. However, in the breeding season, the great white also develops a pink tinge to its feathers from a preen gland.

The bone structure of the pelican is extremely light and permeated with air spaces in between the lightweight bones. These hollow structures make for effective and soaring flight but retain their strength. Moulded into a thin honeycomb effect, the bones are arranged to deal with the stresses of flight. The pelican's breastbone is attached to its pectoral girdle in order to suspend the body from the wings during flight. Designed primarily for agility in the air, the pelican sometimes appears clumsy on the ground, its short, powerful legs being better adapted to swimming than walking. Buoyancy in the sea and the air comes from the air spaces in the body and bones.

Quite a mouthful

The pelican's wide gape is an essential part of its fishing technique, enabling the bird to drop the lower mandible into the water as a fisherman would use a scoop net. At the same time, the bird cannot make more than the slightest lateral movements. If the lower element of the bill were more loosely hinged, it might be dislocated under the pressure of the water and the caught fish.

Inside the bill, the pelican has hardly any tongue at all. It does not cut up the fish or pick at them with the well-developed hook at the tip of its bill, but simply tips back its head and swallows the fish whole. The tough membrane of the gular pouch, hanging below the lower mandible, stretches to accommodate the pelican's catch and the water that comes in with the fish. The pelican's pouch can hold between 13 and 14 litres, but the bird needs ideal conditions before it can take off with so heavy a load.

Paddle feet

The pelican's body, so awkwardly shaped for locomotion on land, is mounted on stout legs and webbed feet. All four toes are webbed, and the inner toe, which in many birds points backwards to give the foot an efficient grasping capability, points forwards, making the pelican's foot a well-shaped paddle.

As light as its bones

For all its size and bulk, the pelican is a relatively light bird. The reason for this paradox is that its body is well supplied with air spaces. Like all birds, the pelican's bones are hollow structures of great strength and lightness, but unlike many birds, the pelican has air spaces in all its bones except its toes.

The hollow interior of the bones is strengthened in the same way as an aeroplane wing, where the lightness and strength are achieved through the use of a thin 'skin' supported by a system of trusses or cross members.

The pelican makes use of thermal currents of air to rise in a spiral to the top of the current where it can maintain sustained soaring flight over a great distance. The inner part of the wings helps to supply lift while the outer half functions as a propelling agent. The outer primary feathers can be altered to brake or accelerate or even twist outwards to attack the air. The primaries lie flat against the wing in gliding flight and can respond to changes in the direction of the wind.

Shaped for lift
The pelican's wing shape, size and lightness make it a superb soaring bird. As the land mass heats up under the sun's rays, the ground gives off heat unevenly, creating updraughts of warm air, called thermals. These mushroom out towards the top rather like the cloud that follows an atomic explosion. The pelicans and other soaring birds fly into these updraughts and glide from thermal to thermal. The birds find this means of staying in the air an extremely economical use of their energy.

	At a glance Eastern white pelican *Pelecanus onocrotalus*
Class	Aves
Subclass	Carinatae
Order	Pelicaniformes
Genus	Pelecanus
Weight	9-12kg
Body length	113-135cm
Bill length	c.35cm
Egg size	80-104 x 52-64.5mm. The eggs are biconal (the same shape at each end).
Incubation period	30-42 days. It is difficult to be accurate about the incubation period because the birds inhabit the nests before, during and after laying, so the laying date is hard to determine precisely.
Clutch	Usually of two, sometimes three, bluish or yellowish eggs, which become coated with a thick, chalky layer, which is white at first but soon discolours.
Chicks	Born naked and blind.
Diet	Mainly of fish with a few crustaceans and occasional small birds.

The Dragonfly

The larks burbled high in the air, mad with songs, as the late July sun rose into the eastern sky. A heavy dew fled from the grass in an hour and even the long grasses under the willows, threaded with bindweed and hawkweed, gleamed with dry polished blades in the sunshine. The willows leaned over the gravel slopes of a wide pond, their leaves trailing like fingers in the calm water. There seemed to be a pause in the scented life of the morning as though the whole natural world were gently breathing in.

The perfect blue of the summer sky was mirrored by the surface of the great pond, here and there interrupted by floating mats of St John's wort, its yellow flowers opening to the sun. Nearby, grew sparse clumps of water milfoil and shore weed. At the southern corner of the pond was an inlet pipe where water dribbled slowly into the still mere. Reaching back from this point flourished a sweep of floating sweetgrass.

The warmth of the sun suffused even the shaded margins of the pond and the surface of the water occasionally shook itself lightly with a delicate flicker of activity as water boatmen, small beetles and gnats began the busy life of the day. Even the birdsong seemed to accompany the picture from a distance, as though the moment were too perfect to touch.

A scintilla of blue, no more than a hint, caught the light, and then there was another sharp flash, as though a strand of spider silk loaded with dew had split a sunbeam into a thread of rainbow light. Again the shard of blue appeared, brighter than the sky and nearer to the shore this time. A needle of blue fire flew fast and straight, parallel to the bank. A moment later it was lost to sight, reappearing to backtrack, and then hovering, poised, a dangerous dart in the air. The thorax shone greenish, burnished like bronze armour and the long abdomen was a brilliant enamelled blue made more startling by a black marking which ran along its length. The wings, a whirr of glistening cuticle, flashed in the light of the morning. The male emperor dragonfly tilted lightly and swung in towards the birch trees beyond the bank.

A few metres to the north of the trees, the golden wings of a large red-brown *Aeshna grandis* patrolled the shaded shallows. The sunlight through the leaves flashed on the segments of his thorax and the light blue-green of his eyes picked out every movement in range. Perhaps it was the flash of sunlight on golden wings that caught the emperor's eyes as he quartered the patrol area, cutting back from the trees towards the pond. He left the shadows like an arrow, dipping slightly to position himself below the interloper, which, in turn, caught the movement at a distance of a dozen metres and rapidly spiralled down to block the upward movement of the attack. Both dragonflies broke away, spiralling down towards the water in parallel, and fencing off any chance of the dangerous upward strike.

The golden-winged intruder shot forwards, close to the water, turned, and turned again, raising his abdomen upwards in a display position. Perhaps this fierce demonstration had been effective in the past, or perhaps he was displaying because he mistook the emperor for a female. Whatever the intention was, the manoeuvre was too slow. For the space of a wingbeat he did not know where the

Opposite page:
This emperor dragonfly, Anax imperator, is perching on a stalk of grass with its silvery, translucent wings outstretched. They are narrow and richly veined, the abdomen is slender and the eyes are prominent. The emperor is easily distinguished from other species of dragonflies by its skewed thorax, striking lapis-lazuli coloured body and forwards pointing legs. In addition, the males have accessory genitalia on the second and third abdominal segments. Anax is a species that is characteristic of spring, and this strikingly coloured dragonfly can be seen skimming the surface of ponds and rivers in the world's warmer, temperate regions.

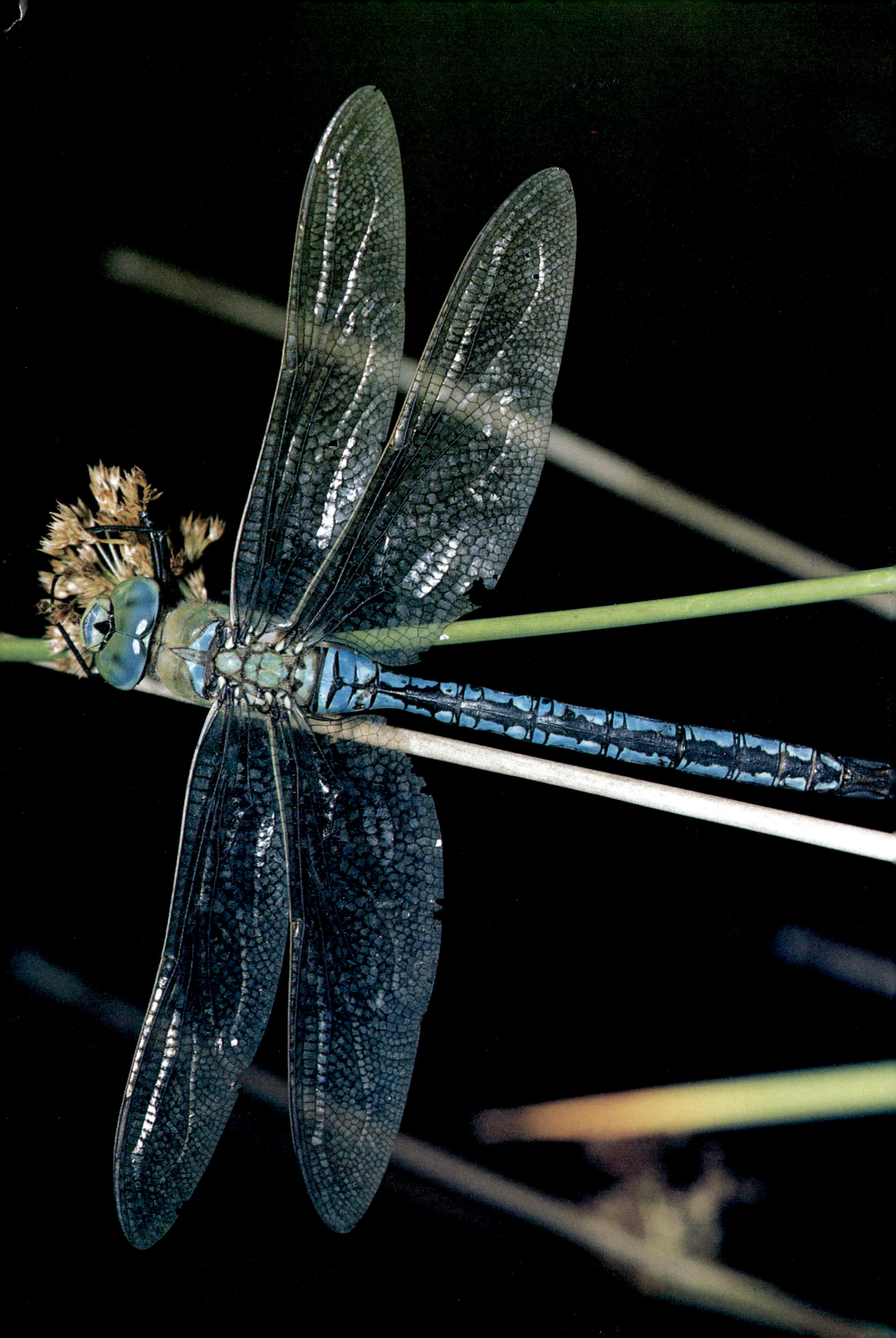

emperor had gone. Almost touching the water, the emperor was beneath him. Flicking sharply upwards, the tough green bronze of the emperor's thorax smashed into the brown dragonfly, damaging one of his wings and spinning him down on his back into the water.

The struggle for lift out of the clinging water, hindered by a maimed wing, wheeled the brown dragonfly about in a flurried circle while the triumphant emperor watched from a few metres away. The brown dragonfly righted himself and was almost clear of the water when a snap of jaws from below caught one beautiful golden wing and began to draw it down into the pale brown water. A crested newt welcomed a good breakfast.

The skirmish seemingly left the emperor unshaken. He hovered for a while and then flew back towards a large willow tree. Here, the weeping fronds made a shady but warm and damp spot especially beloved of gnats. At this time there were none there so the emperor flew with steady wing beats, about 20 to the second, up to the tree tops. He foraged around for some time, avoiding the slower flying birds with ease. Suddenly, a kestrel stooped at his glinting shape, only pulling back at the last moment because the branches of an old pine intervened. This narrow escape sent him darting through the glade to the pond once more.

The midday heat had drawn the gnats to the old willow and the emperor paused at the edge of its dappled shade. The dancing cloud of gnats rose and fell in a swirling column, the sunlight flickering through it. The emperor tore through the middle of the column like a javelin. His wings beating in alternate pairs, his legs drawn forwards to form a scoop which bristled with spurs, he hit his mark and slammed into a large gnat which was just turning towards him. Their combined speeds must have been about 60km per hour. The dragonfly appeared to court disaster by attacking at that speed. At the instant of contact, a ripple seemed to flow along the insect's body. The segments of its thorax, set obliquely to one another, buckled and crumpled at various angles like a compressed spring and then flexed back to their normal position.

These two dragonflies are mating near water in a manner that is unique in the insect world. After the newly adult dragonfly attains sexual maturity, the reproductive period begins and may last up to six weeks. During this time, the males compete in displays and fights for possession of a territory. In order to mate, the male alights on the back of a willing female, holding her head with the claspers at the end of his abdomen. The sperm is transferred from the male accessory organs to the female as she curls herself around the male. The female then flies off to a pond or river to lay her eggs.

The gnat struggled in the grip of the dragonfly's legs but was drawn towards the emperor's mouthparts. The two pairs of jaws dismembered the creature and ground it up. There was no pause in the emperor's flight. He ate on the wing, apparently needing no rest.

He continued the steady patrolling of his 'beat': along the pond's south-eastern bank, a turn towards the matted St John's wort and back to the trees, over to the willow and along the bank again. In the early afternoon, as he sped towards the mat of waterweeds, he saw another dragonfly low down near the yellow flowers. He darted in towards this other strand of blue. The stranger, a female of the same species, flew a little way from the emperor's territory and settled on the stem of a waterweed, while the male hovered nearby. The female's abdomen was in an oddly curled position so that from one side she seemed to make an 'S' shape lying on its side. The male flew in darting movements around her, displaying the brilliance of his appearance and flight.

As he darted and hovered, he bent his abdomen downwards and forwards and turned to pursue the female, which had taken off and was flying fast towards the willow tree. She was near the tree when he caught up with her and dived down on to her back. Claspers on the tenth segment of his body grasped her, slotting precisely into identical depressions in her neck. Together, the dragonflies flew on in tandem, the male appearing to tow the female below and behind him.

This emperor dragonfly female is laying eggs in the long stems of water plants. Some species of dragonflies bury their eggs in gravel or sand at the water's edge or even shed the eggs directly into the water while skimming across the surface with the tip of the abdomen below the water. Some dragonflies even breed in waterfalls and their eggs have a special sticky substance to attach them to moist rocks in areas of dampness and spray. After a short period, the eggs hatch into larvae, or nymphs, which then have to undergo a two-year long process of metamorphosis and skin sheddings before the adult dragonfly emerges.

Briefly, the male hovered beside a drooping twig of willow, then he seized it with his legs and clung to it. His claspers retained their grip on the female while she curved her abdomen forward and under him to reach his sperm pockets. Quivering slightly, the pair mated for just over ten minutes. Then the male let go of the twig, his wings whirring, and the two dragonflies took off together in ecstatic flight.

After some minutes flying in tandem the male released the female and she flew back to the willow tree, pausing here and there to skim a piece of floating debris. She landed on a frond of leaves near the surface of the water. The male darted about her protectively as she used her ovipositor, an egg-laying tube situated in her eighth and ninth segments, to lay some of her eggs. She slit a leaf and pushed the blade-like cone at one end of the egg into the slit, so fixing the egg firmly. She repeated the operation again and again. The injury to the leaf would make it curl in time, giving more protection to the egg buried in its tissue.

Another male dragonfly saw her and flew in close. He seemed attracted to her despite the fact that she was busy laying eggs. However, her recent partner saw the intruder and dived on him, catching him by surprise. The dragonfly fell towards the pond but managed to regain control of his flight in time to flee for open space across the pond.

While the male was diving off the stranger, the female continued neatly depositing her creamy coloured eggs in leaves and plant stems along the shallows of the pond. After an hour or more of following her about, dusk began to fall and it was no longer necessary for the emperor to be so vigilant. Flying off, he would return to protect his territory at dawn.

This emperor dragonfly nymph is carnivorous in its diet, catching its prey by an ingenious method. It remains motionless until a small prey animal, such as a tadpole, young fish or aquatic insect, comes within range. Then, quick as lightning, its long upper lip, the labium, whips out and seizes the prey in pincer-like hooks. The labium is then retracted into the mouth and the prey devoured by the jaws. During the two years it spends as a nymph, the dragonfly may shed its skin eight to 15 times, but finally it climbs on to a water plant and, after a final moult, the winged adult emerges to live out its short lifespan of a few summer months.

This view of a dragonfly perching on a stalk of grass shows its enormous compound eyes which bulge out on both sides of its head. The large eyes are very complex in their structure with between 10,000 and 20,000 facets, each with its own retinal element. A shaft of light is received by each facet from the object it is focusing on to build up a composite image of points of light from all the facets. Thus the more facets that a dragonfly possesses the finer and sharper the resulting image. In this way it can distinguish the form of objects and also perceive them in colour vision.

Dragonflies are seen most often in summer by rivers and ponds. Sometimes known as the 'Devil's darning needle', the dragonfly derives its name from its brilliantly coloured body. It is one of the largest living insects with two pairs of large, slender wings, the membranes of which are supported by a complex system of veins. Below the surface of its slim body are the delicate gills and trachea through which it breathes. Despite its comparatively small size, the dragonfly can fly at speeds of up to 96km/h, although it is able only to flap its wings up and down.

From underwater to the free air

Dragonfly eggs vary in shape from species to species, and are adapted to the conditions under which they are laid, the materials in which they are deposited and the environments in which they incubate. Some dragonflies deposit their eggs directly in the water, and their eggs are adapted to prevent them floating too far from the site of deposition. The *Lestinogomphus africanus* lays its eggs in fast-moving streams. The egg has about 30cm of filament attached to one end. As the egg enters the water, the filament unwinds and becomes entangled in secure growth to act as an anchor. The emperor dragonfly lays an egg with a blade-like cone which the female inserts in the cut that she makes in a leaf or stem. She makes this cut with her ovipositor.

Dragonfly eggs are creamy coloured when they are newly laid, but turn reddish-brown after a day; those that fail to turn brown are infertile. The eggs hatch at widely varied intervals. Laid at an ideal time and in good conditions, the eggs may hatch within 20 days; but if they are laid late in the season, their hatching may be delayed by several months. The delay in the development of the eggs is called diapause. The mechanism of diapause is not understood fully. It is not related directly to temperature but appears to be connected with the season or part of the season when the eggs were laid. Howerer, diapause is an important mechanism for ensuring the survival of the eggs until the season is more suitable for hatching.

Just before the egg hatches, the embryo swallows the amniotic fluid, which helps the insect apply the localised pressure necessary to break the shell. The pre-naiad larva escapes from the egg and, for a while, its legs are pressed close against its elongated body. This stage lasts for a few seconds or several hours before the first moult occurs. A larva's moult is called an ecdysis, and the stages between moults are called instars. A larva may, depending on its species, pass through eight to 15 instars before reaching maturity.

The dragonfly naiad (larva) relies on its eyesight to detect its food, thus choosing moving prey which is easy to spot. At first this consists of microscopic protozoa, such as cyclops and daphnia, but large naiads soon capture small fish and tadpoles. The naiad has a highly developed mask or labium which it can flick forwards to seize its prey between the pincers at the tip. The naiad then chews the victim with its jaws, and finishes the process by grinding it up in a toothed gullet.

The larva crawls about the pond or stream bed to find ambushes for its prey, but it can also squirt water from its rectum and so travel by a form of jet propulsion.

In the final instar, the naiad achieves its full size, staying quite still while the organs inside the larval body change into those of an adult dragonfly. This may take between a fortnight and a month to complete. Its wings form as crumpled tissue inside the naiad's wing pads, and its labium shortens.

Four days before emergence, the larva moves towards the shore and clings to submerged reeds or twigs. It climbs to within 7-15cm of the surface and hangs there waiting. When ready, the naiad climbs out of the water at dusk and, after a few moments, it wriggles its abdomen furiously from side to side. Then it hangs still for about three-quarters of an hour before the cuticle along its back splits open. The dragonfly slowly pulls itself free of its prison and hangs there by its legs.

Five or six hours after leaving the water, the dragonfly suddenly opens its wings as the veins fill with blood. Its abdomen fills with air and liquid is expelled through the anus. Its wings begin to whirr in order to raise its body temperature, and 20 minutes or so later the dragonfly launches itself into the sunshine for its maiden flight.

After about 23 months in the water, during which time the larva of an emperor dragonfly has grown rapidly from about 3mm to over 4.5cm (in its first three months it lengthens by 600 per cent, 50 per cent and 30 per cent) the adult finds itself in an entirely novel environment.

This growth chart shows the metamorphosis from egg to fully developed adult of the emperor dragonfly. The eggs have long filament anchors which unwind in the water to a depth of about 30cm. After leaving the egg, the first instar is spider-like in appearance and feeds on small crustacea and larvae on the bottom. It moults several times, developing wing buds before the adult organs form inside the last skin. This happens after about 23 months, and when these internal changes are complete, the nymph climbs a reed stem above the surface of the water and waits for the final moult. The cuticle soon bursts and the adult dragonfly begins to pull itself free, drawing its abdomen clear of the larval skin and hanging from the skin by its legs. At this stage, its wings are still crumpled but they soon fill with air and blood to complete the insect's metamorphosis.

Head of dragonfly nymph

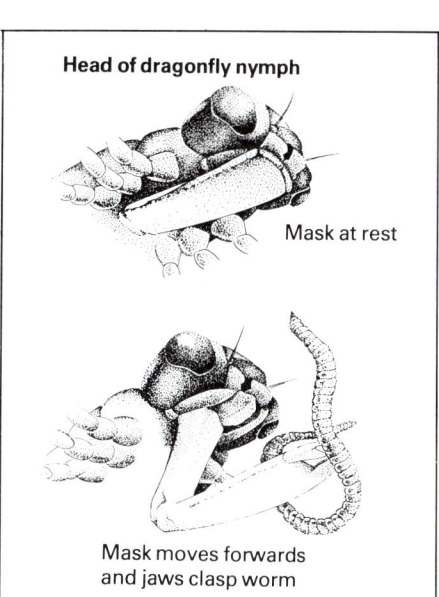

Mask at rest

Mask moves forwards and jaws clasp worm

These two views of the mask of a dragonfly nymph show it at rest and moving forwards to clasp a worm. When a prey animal draws near to the nymph, it strikes with its labium extended, opening its prehensile lower lip. At the tip of the labium are tiny hooks which grasp the victim securely before it is pulled back into the nymph's mouth to be eaten by the mandibles. When the labium is extended, blood pressure, which is controlled by the abdominal diaphragm, is increased. In the resting position, the labium is folded beneath the thorax and head in such a way that it hides the lower half of the face, thus causing it to be called a 'mask' by many scientists.

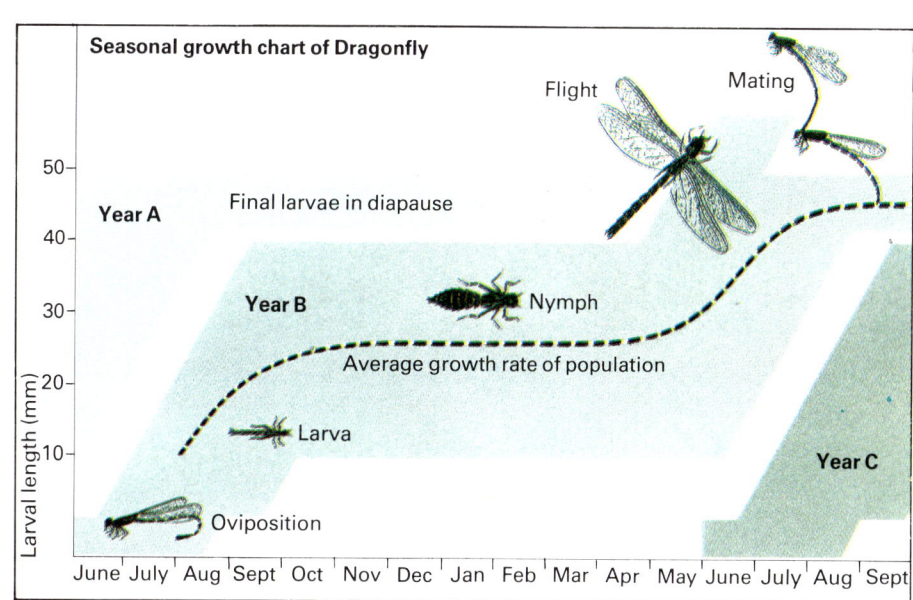

Seasonal growth chart of Dragonfly

Flight — Mating
Year A — Final larvae in diapause
Year B — Nymph
Average growth rate of population
Larva
Oviposition
Year C

Larval length (mm): 50, 40, 30, 20, 10

June | July | Aug | Sept | Oct | Nov | Dec | Jan | Feb | Mar | Apr | May | June | July | Aug | Sept

This seasonal growth chart for the dragonfly is based on scientific research and pond surveys. The dotted line approximates to the average growth of the given pond's population of larvae. The survey was carried out in southern England and therefore the seasonal dates apply to that area in the northern hemisphere. Most of the larval group enter their final instar in August and September, a year after hatching. They emerge in the subsequent year after wintering in the diapause. A small group of precocious larvae miss the diapause, however, and emerge later in the same year. Thus the whole metamorphosis may take many months, sometimes as much as two years, before the adult dragonfly emerges.

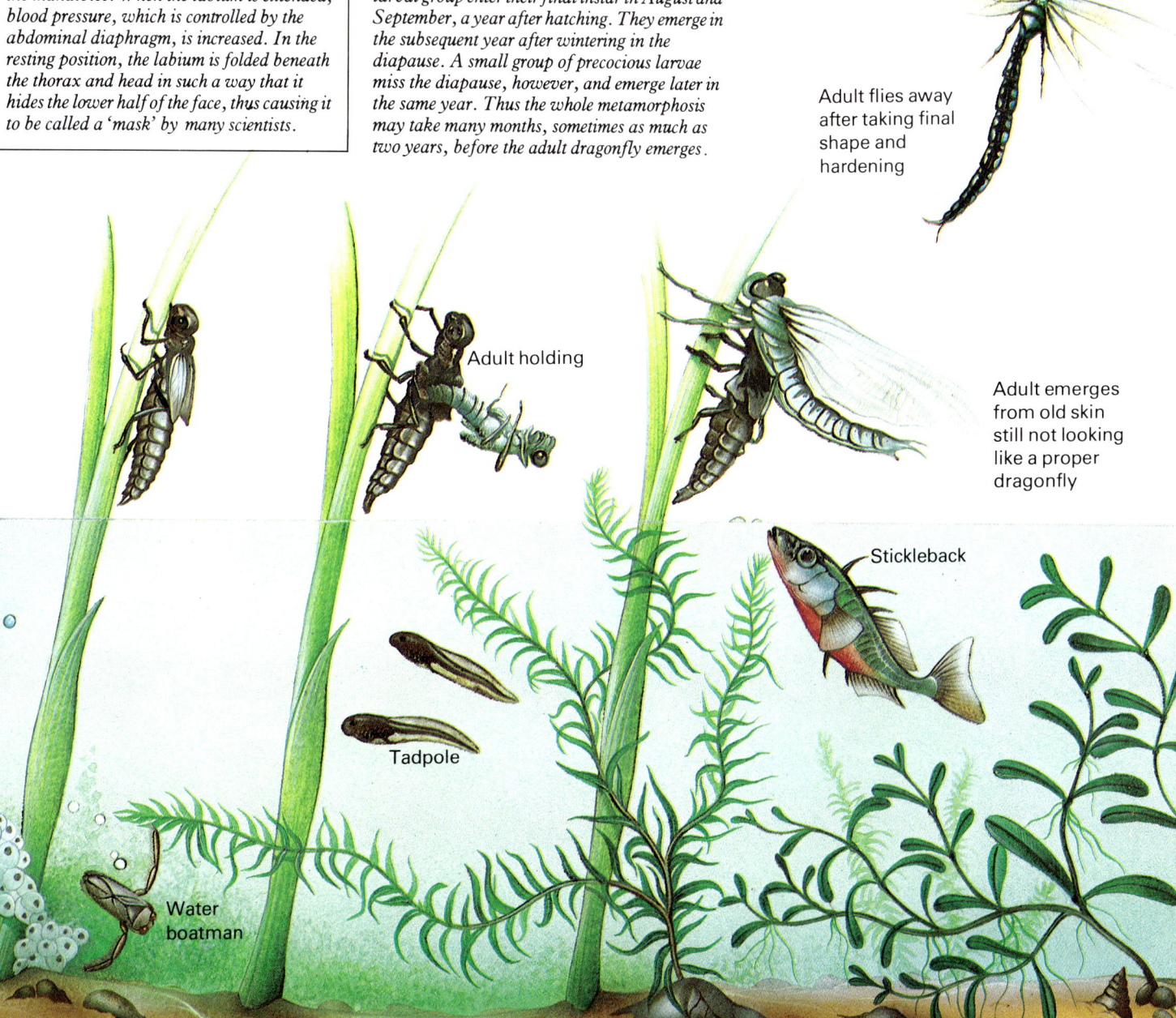

Adult flies away after taking final shape and hardening

Adult holding

Adult emerges from old skin still not looking like a proper dragonfly

Stickleback

Tadpole

Water boatman

Libellula depressa

Aeshna grandis

Cordulia linaenea

Cordulegaster boltonii

Some of the many colourful species of dragonflies are illustrated here. Although it is found in most parts of the world, the dragonfly is particularly common in tropical regions. It is one of the fastest members of the insect world, reaching speeds of nearly 100km/h and changing direction so quickly that it can deceive the human eye. Over the centuries the dragonfly has captured the imaginations of poets and writers with its brilliant colours and darting flight. In some parts of England it is known as a 'horse stringer' or 'adder-bolt'. Some of the larger species are called 'mosquito hawks' in North America. They inhabit many streams, watercourses and rivers and some species are even specialised for breeding in waterfalls, marshes and the water in leaves.

At a glance		
Emperor dragonfly		
Anex imperator		
Class	Insecta
Order	Odonata
Sub-order	Anisoptera
Family	Aeshnidae
Length head to tail	c. 7.5cm
Wing length	c.4.5cm
Colour	Thorax of metallic green, and abdomen in blue and black.
Head	Mobile and equipped with two pairs of jaws assisted by hooks at the sides of the head.
Eyesight	Good monocular and binocular vision. Can distinguish moving objects at 20m.
Flight speed	Up to 50 km/h.
Eggs	Females lay up to 100 eggs in plant stems.
Naiad	The naiad lives in the water. Metamorphosis is completed when the naiad climbs from the water, and the dorsal part of its thorax splits open.
Lifespan	2 to 3 years.

Anax imperator

Aeshna juncea

Orteptrum cancellatum

Syneptrum sanguineum

This golden ringed dragonfly, Cordulegaster boltoni, *is resting on a grass stem. Its brilliantly striped black and yellow body is long and slender and its translucent silvery wings are outstretched in a characteristic position. This dragonfly is a member of the* Anisoptera *suborder and is a northern genera. The* Anisoptera *are distinguished from the* Zygoptera *by their larger bodies and broad hind wings. Swift and agile in flight, they are highly manoeuvrable and can even hover, unlike most other insects. Their wings are laterally extended when they are resting.*

The close-up view shows a dragonfly's head with cut-away sections through the compound eye and transparent cuticle. Inside the cuticle, the ommatidia, or visual units, fit together like a series of cells in a honey-comb. Each functions independently, light being transmitted down the rhabdon (retinal rod) after passing through the lens. A special pigment barrier of cells screens the ommatidium from stray light. The compound eyes themselves are less than one eye-width apart and sometimes touch across the head's centre.

The dragonfly's eyes

The insect's compound eye collects light through thousands of lenses — up to 28,000 in large dragonflies. Each lens picks up an image in its field of vision, but there are two sensors in the ommatidium that leads to the nerves to register details. It is only the light intensity that is 'seen'. A pigment barrier round each ommatidium screens out the light from its neighbours in order that a complex series of light intensity messages is fed to the insect's brain.

The consequent mosaic of light appears like the negative of an image printed in a newspaper. Instead of the newsprint picture of black dots on white paper, the insect sees an image made of points of light of greater or lesser intensity. This theory of insect vision, called the mosaic theory, was first expounded by Johannes Müller in 1829 and, with some modification of its details, still stands as an explanation.

The function of the dragonfly's eyes is supported by three ocelli, lying in a triangular pattern between the insect's eyes. These ocelli consist of a window of transparent cuticle which covers the nerve cells of the retina. It is believed that the ocelli operate as secondary light-sensitive organs, helping the insect find some suitable light conditions independently of its eyes. Certainly, some insects move to ideal light conditions even when their eyes are covered.

Weapons for the hunter

The dragonfly depends, like a hawk, on its agile, fast flight and its capacity to pick out prey effectively. Its four wings are adapted to the type of flight that the species needs. Some dragonflies fly through the obstacle-strewn environment of the jungle, and have paddle-shaped wings to help them achieve the twisting, dodging flight pattern at low speeds demanded by that situation. Others, living in open riverine areas where high speed is more valuable than agility, have long, narrow, rather pointed wings.

Fast and darting flight while searching for insect prey requires acute eyesight if the dragonfly is to be successful and if it is to avoid accidents. The insect eye is a compound instrument capable of a wide angle of vision. The dragonfly can turn its head in flight, and its large projecting eyes give it a good view above, below, to the sides and even, to some extent, to the rear. The insect's sight range is

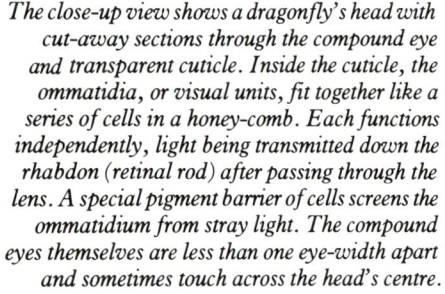

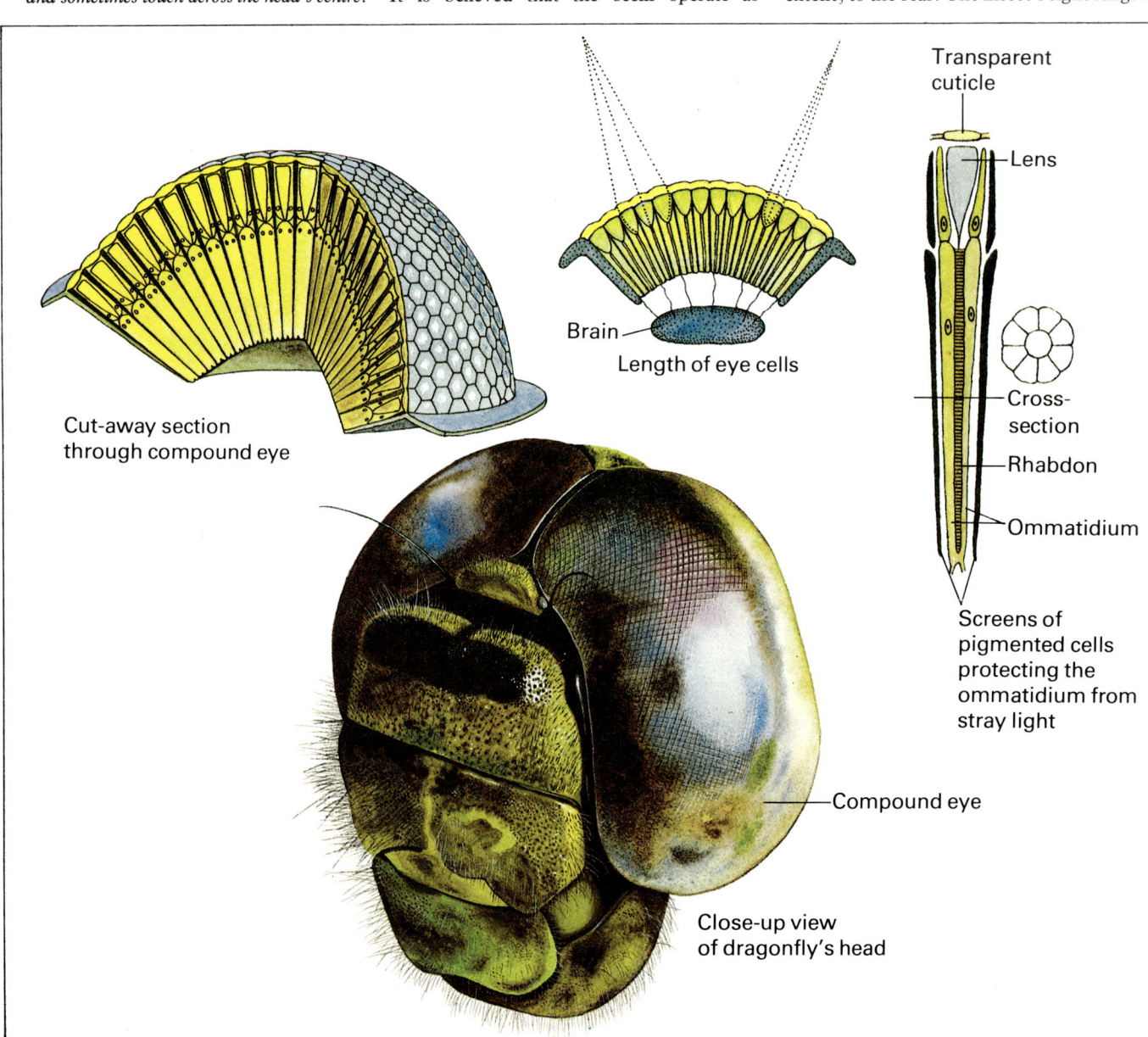

Cut-away section through compound eye

Brain
Length of eye cells

Transparent cuticle
Lens
Cross-section
Rhabdon
Ommatidium
Screens of pigmented cells protecting the ommatidium from stray light

Compound eye
Close-up view of dragonfly's head

short — it can distinguish shapes at a range of five to six metres, and can detect movements at 15 to 20 metres, but if one relates this length of vision to the speed of flight, one realises how remarkable is the nervous system that interprets the visual information and translates it into swift reactions to avoid disaster and seize prey on the wing.

The dragonfly's wings
The dragonfly's two pairs of wings can operate independently, to produce very fast flight, to make quick darting turns, and to allow the insect to hover. They can lock into position also for an energy-saving glide. The dragonfly's flying wizardry is essential to its role as a winged predator.

Its wing consists of a very thin double layer of cuticle attached to the second and third segments of the thorax. The fabric of the wing is held rigid by a grid of fine tubes called veins, through which the wings are supplied with nerve responses, air and blood. The grid varies from species to species, but insects of one species have the same arrangement of veins in their wings, a useful means of identification and classification for entomologists.

A dragonfly, like other flying insects, has a wing shape with a stout leading edge which tapers to a fine edge at the back. Its shape resembles an aeroplane's wing, and its concave underside and convex top surface give it lift. The leading edge can be inclined at an angle to increase lift, and the wing may be twisted in flight to assist in steering the insect.

The wing beat of the dragonfly, at about 20 beats per second, is slow for an insect, but with four wings of similar size and an effective overall aerodynamic shape, it is the fastest of insects. Its style of flight is not as flexible as that of many other insects, such as the bee, but it hovers well and can glide for long distances.

The muscles that operate the wings lie within the thorax. One set of muscles contract to sweep the wings upwards whereas another set draw the wings down again.

When the dragonfly glides, it is using the same principles as those of a man-made glider. A dragonfly cannot fold its wings and holds them outstretched when relaxing. When it glides, the dragonfly's wings are locked into this outstretched position. The insect glides more or less into the wind, its forward motion supplying the 'wing' in still air.

Here, the vein pattern of the dragonfly's wing is shown in addition to the mechanics of a dragonfly's flight. Long and slender and aerodynamically designed, the dragonfly's wing is held firm by a fine network of veins which supply it with essential air and blood and carry nerve responses to the brain. The wings are raised up and down in flight, the muscles in the thorax contracting on the upward strokes and relaxing on the downward strokes. When the insect glides into the wind, its wings are held outstretched and horizontal to its body. The pull of gravity is proportional to the insect's body weight as is the degree of drag, the air displaced by flight. As the dragonfly flies, it tilts its wing to make a shallow dive and to maintain its momentum.

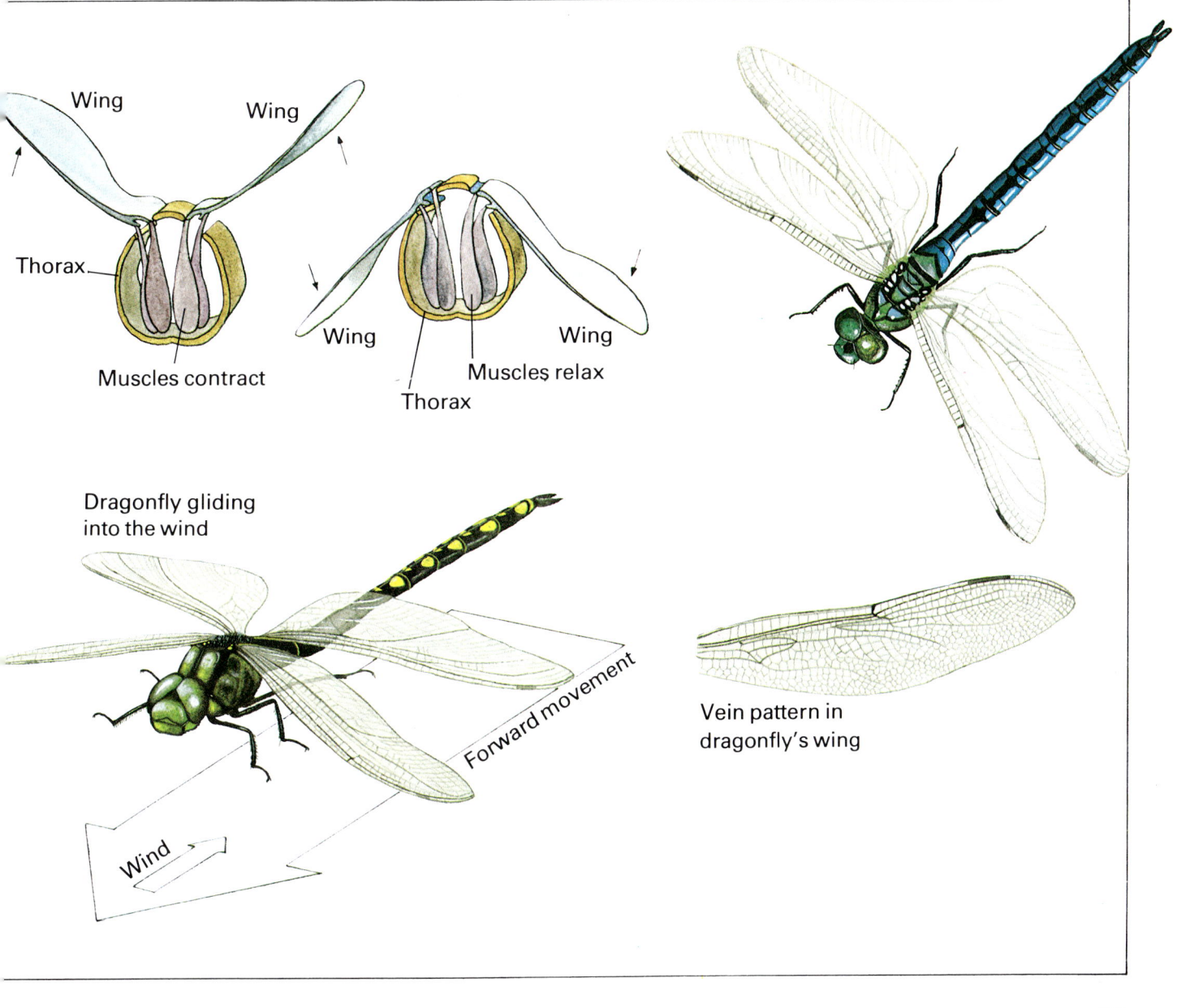

The Whale

Cold morning drizzle roughened the undulating swell to a matt grey. The world seemed to have no edges as the horizon's rim was lost in a gradual softening of the leaden colour of the moving water, and from above more water fell softly down. The wind swirled and teased the rain into slowly dancing veils, while the waves heaved with hardly a break for a briefly foaming head to whiten them.

Eyes that were used to the seas and their changing patterns would, after a while, detect a strangely smooth 'pathway' across the ocean. The 'path' was not still. It swelled and rolled with the movement of the sea but there was a distinct oiliness, a smoothness in the texture of the surface of the water, leading the gaze into the distance. The 'way' seemed to speak of purpose and suggested the mark of a living creature.

A watery yellow wash that was all that could be seen of the sun, nearly overwhelmed by the grey drizzle, began to suck away the saturated air. The 'path' looked clearer where the light reflected from it. It was unlike a wake. No side-wash of ripples and waves fanned out from it, more a curling down of the water at its sides. At the point where the path seemed to lead, the sea opened to reveal a blunt, square-bowed head which announced its presence a moment later with a tall plume of vapour that arched three or four metres upwards and out to the left. The soft yellow light shone on the dark grey head of the mighty old sperm whale, a lighter grey than the near black of his youth, as he forged steadily through the sea's surface waters for about five minutes.

Every 20 seconds or so he blew away the mixture of air, emulsion and mucus from the single nostril that opened briefly on the upper left side of his head. He took only two or three seconds to suck in lungsful of air and to blow away the used air and oils, then he would pause before taking the next breath, disappearing for about 12 seconds before emerging to breathe again. After five minutes of this rapid breathing, he dipped his head deep and the seas closed over him. For 20 minutes the oily pathway crossed the ocean before the dark head emerged again.

The old male had spent a lonely summer deep in Antarctic waters. He had seen only two whales of his own kind in those long

Female sperm whales, their young and attendant males often live in large groups, or 'pods', which sometimes number several hundred animals. Bulls without a harem usually travel alone, especially in polar waters when the breeding season is over. The largest of the toothed whales, sperm whales are found in all oceans of the world but live in warmer, tropical seas when breeding. Darkish grey on its back and with a paler grey or white belly, the sperm whale's huge head accounts for about one-third of its total body length. It is a deepwater species, rarely found in depths of less than 100m and often diving to 500m or more to search for its favourite food — the giant squid, which forms a major part of its diet. Old whales often bear white scars on their heads resulting from their encounters and battles with the squid.

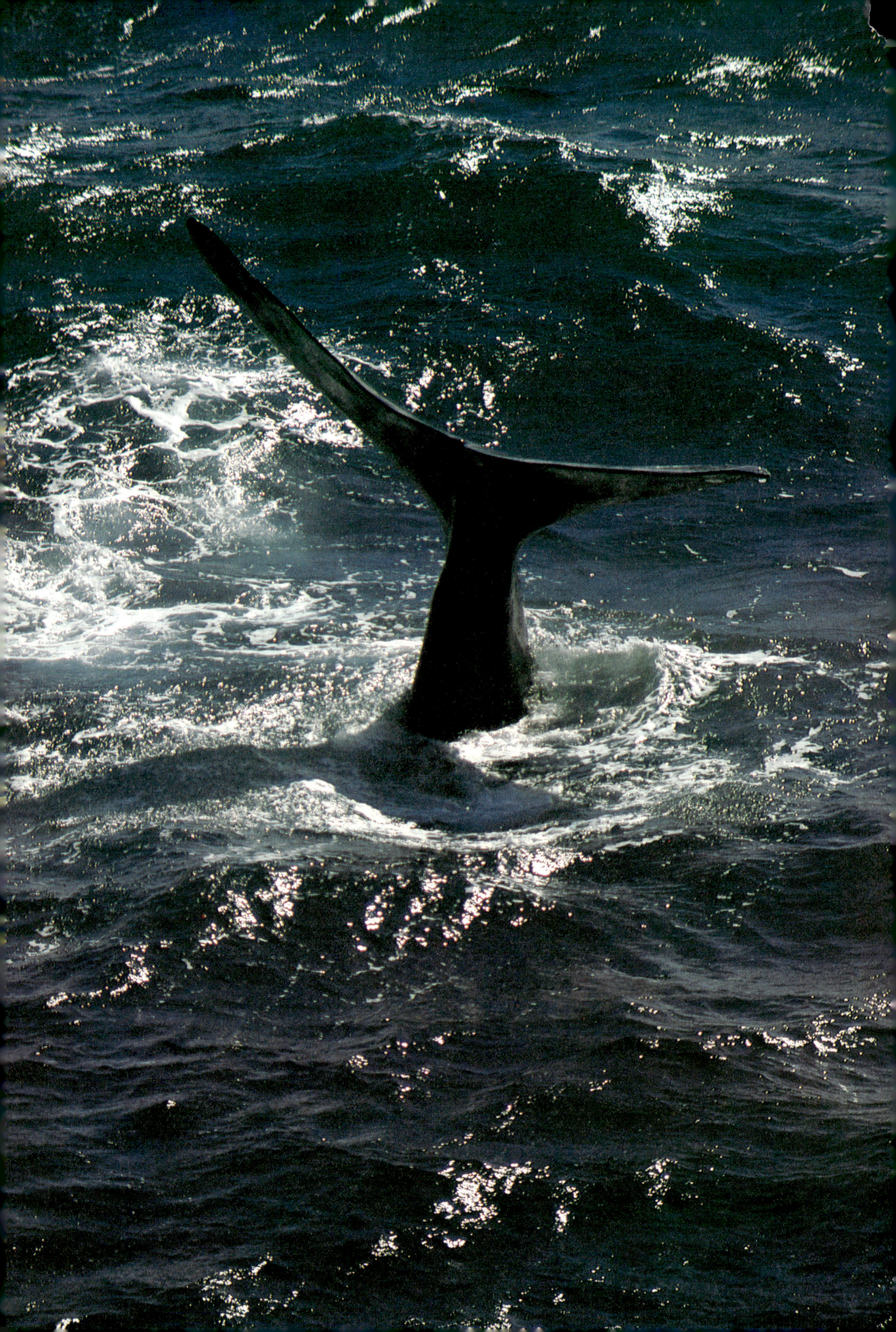

months. They, too, had been old, almost as battle-scarred as he. His massive head was pitted with the marks left by some of the large prey that he had taken in his jaws. His long, slender lower jaw was deeply puckered about one-third of the way from its point. The angle of the jaws changed where the bone on the right side had fractured. Two years earlier, he had met the spring challenge of a bull whale who was as powerful as himself, and lost. The jaw had knitted strongly but slightly askew.

Plunging deep under the surface of the sea, the sperm whale moved with a slow, graceful bucking motion. He sent out clicking sounds and listened for the return. Instinctively, he sorted the information, responses from layers of cold water, and – suddenly – came the response he was seeking. He turned with a supple twist of his huge bulk and the great flukes swept up and down to drive him more swiftly through the water. There, moving across his line of approach was a large school of hake. His jaw gaping wide, he swept through the school, grasping the fine silver fish and swallowing them whole. The school fled this way and that while the sperm whale smashed his way through their tight formation and gobbled up its members by the dozen. The whale drove himself to the surface for air, the edge taken from his appetite.

While he restocked his air supply and rid himself of spermaceti and water, he looked around the ocean. His eyesight was short-ranged, but his curiosity about some faint sounds he had received from a deep hunting dive during the previous night kept him alert. He was hungry for the company of females of his own species. It had been two years now since he had swum the ocean with his own harem about him and a long time since he had mated.

He breathed in and out quickly, several times, to store a good supply of air for a deep dive. He jack-knifed down, lobtailing his flukes clear of the water. Bucking down through the water, with a force equivalent to nearly 500 horsepower, his eyesight was soon useless. The darkness of the depths forced him to depend on his

Opposite page:
This southern right whale, E. australis, is swimming off the Argentinian coast in the Golfo San José with its tail raised vertically out of the water. The right whales derive their name from the old whalers in the nineteenth century who considered them to be the right whales to catch. They were prized for their baleen plates and oil. Owing to extensive whaling activities in the Pacific and Atlantic oceans, however the right whales, especially the black and Greenland species, are now becoming rare.

This aerial view shows the difference in size between a boat and a southern right whale and calf, whose combined bulk dwarfs the boat. Right whales are very large and may grow up to 15m in length. They are unusual among whalebone whales in that they have no dorsal fin or grooves on the underside of the throat. The large, bizarrely shaped mouth contains about 600 plates of whalebone and the upper jaw is powerfully arched to incorporate these large plates.

This southern right whale is breaching the Peninsula Valdes in Argentina, leaping right out of the water. Right whales can stay submerged below water for periods of up to 60 minutes. They sleep on the surface and are heavy sleepers, as sometimes the noise of a ship's engine will fail to awaken them from their slumbers. They have a sense of social duty towards each other and often the males will help and support weak, sick or injured females. The right whale has about 250 whiskers on its chin and the tip of the upper jaw which are well-supplied with blood and nerve fibres. Obviously, they have an important sensory role to play although this is still not fully understood.

superb faculty of echolocation. His clicks returning to him 'read' the water ahead of him and around him – a new response, not the one he had been listening for, but a welcome one. Plunging down towards it, he knew the object was large and the character of the responses were ones he had often heard before, though the creature he was homing in on was bigger than any he had found for several years.

The sperm whale inclined his dorsal fins to plane into a shallower dive. The responses were strong now and he was in the darkness, 350 metres below the wave-tossed surface. His enormous jaw hung open, faintly pallid in the dimness, as he glided in towards his prey. There it was, the tough, three and a half-metre cylinder of a giant squid's body. Its long tentacles reached, almost lazily, to wrap themselves round the whale's lower jaw. The whale's jaws clenched tight on the hard body, and he bucked hard for the surface. The pressure of the water on his barrel-shaped body became less and less as he swept upwards, moving fast. His great burden lashed out with the club-like sucker pads on the ends of its long arms, gouging wounds in the whale's great head. The tentacles clung round the whale's jaws as the squid tried to pry those terrible teeth away from its body. The whale's huge snout suffered the onslaught of the squid's arms, but the eyes and other vital organs were hard to find. There were no gills to rip at, and the very size of the whale made it impossible to immobilise by simply wrapping it up as the squid might have done with a lesser prey.

The struggle was now near the surface of the sea, and the squid's senses were succumbing to the effects of the nitrogen bubbles fizzing through its blood vessels as it rapidly decompressed. The whale had rarely had to struggle so long before. He wrenched his head from side to side to tear his prey apart, and still the squid's horny beak ripped and teared. With a last surge of his flukes, the whale thrust himself half out of the water and fell back with a smashing blow that tore the squid apart.

The whale blew. His plume of spray was tinged with blood from the deep, gouging wounds where the squid had slashed at his nostril. His damage was slight if seen in relation to his bulk, but he was more than 40 years old so he took his time recovering his energy before breaking up the remains of the squid into manageable mouthfuls.

The sperm whale rested, lying still in the water and looking rather like a shoal with the swell covering and uncovering his back. Late in the afternoon, he began to swim steadily towards the sounds he had heard earlier. Swimming along the surface for much of the time, the lower part of his snout – where it was narrowest – cut through the water cleanly. The sonar responses were a little confused, but the clicks of a sperm whale herd were nearer. The light was still clear when he actually saw the faint cloud of a whale's blow and then another.

He swam more powerfully now but never with any appearance of haste. A creature as large as he, and one embodying such power, was never ungainly or ungraceful in the element to which he had adapted so completely.

At last he approached close enough to the herd to see that it was made up of several mature females and a few immature males of two or three years of age. He swam in a gentle arc to meet the herd, uttering deep groaning calls, and the herd turned towards him. He lunged upwards to drive his head high out of the water, fanning his

The killer whale is closely related to the pilot and false killer whales, and although it is classified generally as a whale it is not a true whale. Its striking markings, shiny black on top and white underneath, make it instantly recognisable. Found in all seas, especially in the Arctic and Antarctic regions, the killer whale lives and hunts in large packs and has few enemies. It has a voracious appetite and is the only cetacean that will hunt warm-blooded creatures, such as penguins, seals and dolphins. The other prey that makes up its varied diet includes porpoises, fish, squid and even other whales. It is not uncommon for a group of killers to attack and eat a whale larger than themselves. They catch seals and penguins unawares by gliding silently below an ice floe on which their prey is sitting and tilting the mass of ice with their heads. They prey is caught neatly as it is tipped off the ice into the cold sea.

The tails and fins of these whales are silhouetted against the sea in Glacier Bay off the coast of Alaska. Whales are descended from four-footed mammals that lived on land about 65 million years ago. They took to the sea in the Palaeocene era and adapted to their new aquatic environment. The whale is specialised for its watery existence with a streamlined body, tapering gradually towards the tail, for fast, powerful movement through the sea, and pointed, flat tail flukes to provide propulsive power when swimming. Like other mammals, it needs to breathe air, which is inhaled and exhaled through a blowhole on top of its head. This specialised nasal opening is located behind the snout and allows the whale to breathe when the rest of its body is submerged.

flukes so that he stood straight and high for several seconds. He saw the herd bucking through the waves towards him and beyond them a school of fish leaping from the water, desperate to avoid the herd. The whales had already had their fill and were breaking away to deeper water again, nervous of what lay beyond the fish. All this the old sperm whale saw with his bright black eyes, and in the distance a dark line of land.

From the landward side of the herd swam the powerful form of the herd's bull whale. At a closing speed of nearly 40 knots the two great bulls surged towards each other. The clash was inevitable. Closer and closer the 60-tonne giants raced while the herd gathered a little way off to watch the encounter.

At the last moment, the whales veered slightly in an effort to attack each other's flanks. The old bull managed to give the younger whale a glancing blow but it had little effect. They circled one another, searching for advantage. The young whale surged in with a charge that caught the old bull on the side of the head, well back. The blow was not heavy enough to injure his head but for a while he could not see and was momentarily stunned. Taking the advantage the young whale turned onto the old bull's back. There was no time for the old bull to turn the attack. The young bull drove his lower jaw hard into the deep scar of the old jaw fracture and hung on. The water sucked and frothed on the surface as the two lashed and twisted their gigantic bodies in this death struggle.

An awful crack and a harsh bellow from the old whale signalled the end of the fight. His jaw hanging loosely, he tried to break away, but for a while the young bull hung on. With a fearsome swipe of his tail, he let his disabled opponent go. He drove him away from the herd with butting charges that thudded home on the old whale's sides. A last slap with the terrible four-metre tail flukes, this time across his snout, and the defeated sperm whale struggled clear of his last battle.

The herd swam seawards to the deep water that was their secure home. The old bull swam blindly for a while and then drifted as he tried to sort out the responses of his sonar. The sun had sunk below the western horizon and the sea was dark with rain again. The fight had driven him close to the muddy outflow of a river and he now wearily swam on towards the shore. He swam on the surface now for much of the time, breathing often. With his remaining good eye, he saw the danger in the silhouette of the low rocks against the sky. He turned quickly. The mud of the river mouth caught him under the belly. It was soft but clinging. He swept his flukes down to drive himself forward, and gained a few feet, then stuck fast.

By midmorning the tide had fallen. The old whale lay high and dry, beached in the warm sun. The blubber that had insulated him from the Antarctic cold failed to protect him now. He was desperately hot. The wounds that he had suffered attracted gulls who pecked at them. More than anything else, he was exhausted by the effort of breathing and of resisting the dreadful pressure of his own weight. His bulk, no longer supported by the sea, leaned in on his organs. He groaned and listened. There was no response, his wonderful sonar system was not functioning without the water as a carrier of its messages.

Slowly, he became comatose. The once mighty ocean traveller that had feared no other creature and could swim beneath the worst storms collapsed in on himself. The weight and size that had made him master of his element now defeated him, and, heaving out a last sigh, he died.

The beluga whale (below left) is among the smallest whales and lives in northern seas. A relative of the narwhal, it grows to about 5.5m in length. The whale's mouth (below right) is extremely large to accommodate the enormous amounts of sea water that it must swallow when feeding. A large part of the mouth is made up of the baleen, a whalebone filter for sorting out particles of food. Crustacea and other food are filtered through the whalebone fringes in the mouth. These individual plates are rooted inside the upper jaw and are lowered when feeding to strain the 'krill', small, shrimp-like creatures, from the water. When the whale closes its mouth the plates are raised.

Whales with teeth

In the world today there are two main types of whale: those with teeth and those without. Whales that have no teeth have a mass of fringed boney plates which act as filters for the plankton that forms their diet. The plates are called baleen, and baleen whales are generally faster and larger than toothed whales.

Toothed whales (*Odontoceti*) live in all oceans and vary greatly in size and shape. The *Odontoceti* include dolphins and porpoises as well as whales, but this survey of the toothed whales concentrates on those animals that consistently exceed three and a half metres in length.

True's beaked whale (*Mesoplodon mirus*) and **Sowerby's whale** (*M. bidens*) are similar in shape. *M. mirus* is between three and seven metres long. It travels singly or in schools, and feeds on squid, octopus and fish in deep waters. Its gestation period is about 12 months, and it breeds in spring or late winter. Two teeth develop at the front of the mouth of True's beaked whale, whereas they appear at the side of the mouth of Sowerby's beaked whale. The underside of *M. mirus* is a light grey and speckled, but *M. bidens* is dark grey.

There are about ten species of the *Mesoplodon* family. There are found mainly in the temperate waters of both hemispheres.

Cuvier's beaked whale (*Ziphius cavirostris*) grows to between 5.5 and 8.5 metres, and weighs over 1 600kg. Its pectoral fins are about 0.5m and the dorsal fins about 3.05cm. The tail flukes are 1.5m across. Cuvier's beaked whales commonly swim in schools of 30 to 40, feeding on octopus, squid and fish. They are found in warm and temperate seas in both hemispheres. Their gestation period is about 12 months.

The **Tasmanian beaked whale** (*Tasmacetus sheperdi*) is rare, and is known only from a few standard specimens found off the coast of New Zealand. It appears to grow to about five metres with a long beak containing 90 teeth.

Baird's beaked whale (*Beradius bairdi*) is 9 to 12m long and swims in schools of about 20. Its pectoral fins are one metre long and the dorsal fin is 3.05cm high. Its flukes are 2.5 to 3m across. *B. bairdi* is found in the eastern and western parts of the north Pacific as far north as the Bering Sea. It feeds on squid, octopus, rockfish and herring. It can be distinguished at sea by the habit of raising its flukes to dive. Its back is brownish-black and the underside is of the same colour but marked with splashes of white. It has a gestation period of about 10 months.

Of the same family is Arnoux's beaked whale (*B. arnouxi*), but it is found in the Antarctic Ocean. It grows to between 9.8 and 10.5m long and calves in August usually.

The **bottle-nosed whale** (*Hyperoodon ampullatus*) measures seven to nine metres in length. It is blackish in colour when young and grows paler with age. The males, which are larger than the females, have two teeth in their lower jaws. Bottle-nosed whales travel in schools of four to 12. They frequently leap clear of the water and dive at great speed. In the days of hand-harpooning from open boats, this habit proved dangerous to whalers. The whale will not desert an injured companion but swims beside it protectively. In summer, the bottle-nosed whales are found in the North Atlantic, where their young are born from May to June, and in the winter the schools migrate to the Mediterranean. The southern bottle-nosed whale, *Hyperoodon planifrans*, is a similar animal found in the temperate and cold waters of the southern hemisphere.

The **sperm whale** (*Physeter catodon*) is the greatest of the toothed whales. See *At a glance* panel.

The **pygmy sperm whale** (*Kogia breviceps*) is a subfamily — with only one genus and species — of the *Physeteridae* family of sperm whales. The pygmy sperm whale grows 2.75-4m long and weighs 180-320kg. Its flukes are about 6.2cm wide. Its lower jaw has nine to 15 teeth on each side, well adapted to catching the cuttle fish, squid, crabs and prawns that form its diet. The pygmy sperm whale breeds in the warm waters of the Atlantic, Pacific and Indian oceans in winter and migrates to polar waters in the summer. It has a gestation period of about nine months.

The **narwhal** (*Monodon monoceros*) grows to a length of up to 4.5m and is closely related to the beluga whale. With age, it becomes whitish with dark blotches on its back. One of its teeth develops into a tusk which projects as much as 2.4m from the upper lip of a male narwhal. The use of the tusk is uncertain. The animal is found principally in the North Atlantic within the Arctic Circle.

Killer whale (*Orcinus orca*) males may grow up to 9.14m, and females grow to about seven metres. The male has a 1.8m dorsal fin that stands up characteristically on its back. The female's dorsal fin is smaller and more backwards sloping. Killer whales travel in large schools and are the only whales known to attack and eat other whales and to include seals in their diet, but the bulk of their food consists of fish. They are extremely intelligent animals, which makes them hard to catch.

False killer whale (*Pseudorca crassidens*) males grow to six metres and weigh up to 1.5 tonnes, but females grow to only 4.75m. The false killer whale's dorsal fin is more backwards inclined than that of the true killer whale. Its teeth, between 32 and 44 of them, are circular in section, not oval as are those of *O. orca*. The false killer whale moves about in schools of several hundred animals, eating cephalopods and many species of fish.

The **pilot whale** (*Globicephala melaena*) grows to a length of between 3.5 and eight metres, and travels in schools of several hundred. It is named for its habit of 'follow the leader'. Pilot whales are armed with 28 to 44 teeth. They live in all oceans but are not found in polar seas. Females mature at about six years and become barren at around 18 years. The gestation period is about 12 months. Bulls mature much later, at 13 years. Between 3,000 and 4,000 pilot whales are killed each year off the Newfoundland coast in summer, and many others in the Faroes. Another species, *G. scammoni*, is found in the north Pacific Ocean.

The **beluga, or white, whale** (*Delphinapterus leucas*) grows to between 3.75 and 4.25m long, males being generally 30cm longer than females. Their gestation period lasts about 14 months, and when the calf is born it is about 1.5m long and of a blackish hue. For the next two years it grows one metre per year, then the rate of growth slows down and the animal's skin becomes paler until by the age of about five years it is white. The beluga has 10 teeth in the upper jaw and 16 in the lower one. It inhabits Arctic waters, entering shallow bays and even swimming up rivers. In harsh winters it migrates to the south. The beluga's diet is of fish and crustaceans.

There is no formal definition of what actually constitutes a whale and thus it is customary to consider any animal in the order that includes whales, dolphins and porpoises larger than about six and a half metres in length as a whale. Although true dolphins, the killer and pilot whales are called whales because of their large size. When fully grown, the pygmy whale just reaches 6.5m. The largest of the toothed whales, the sperm whale has an enormous, square head which makes up a third of its total body length of 18m. The beaked and bottle-nosed whales, inhabitants of northern seas, are also true species of whale. All whalebone whales are highly developed for the method of filter feeding on small crustaceans.

Sperm whale

Elephant   Man

Here, a sperm whale is compared in size with an elephant and a man. The largest mammal in the animal world, the sperm whale is 18m long with an enormous head, which contains a high reservoir filled with clear spermaceti oil, which solidifies on contact with the air.

Curvier's whale

Pilot whale

Bottle-nosed whale

Killer whale

Pygmy sperm whale

White beluga whale

Sperm whale

Narwhal

True's beaked whale

Sowerby's whale

False killer whale

113

This killer whale is performing tricks at an aquarium in San Diego, California. Whales are extremely intelligent creatures and can be trained to perform before audiences, leaping high out of the water to catch fish and even jumping through flaming hoops. Sometimes they become very tame, truly co-operating with their trainers and being fed by hand. However, they are aggressive killers in the wild, hunting in packs to satisfy their voracious appetite and eating fellow whales if they are injured or smaller than themselves.

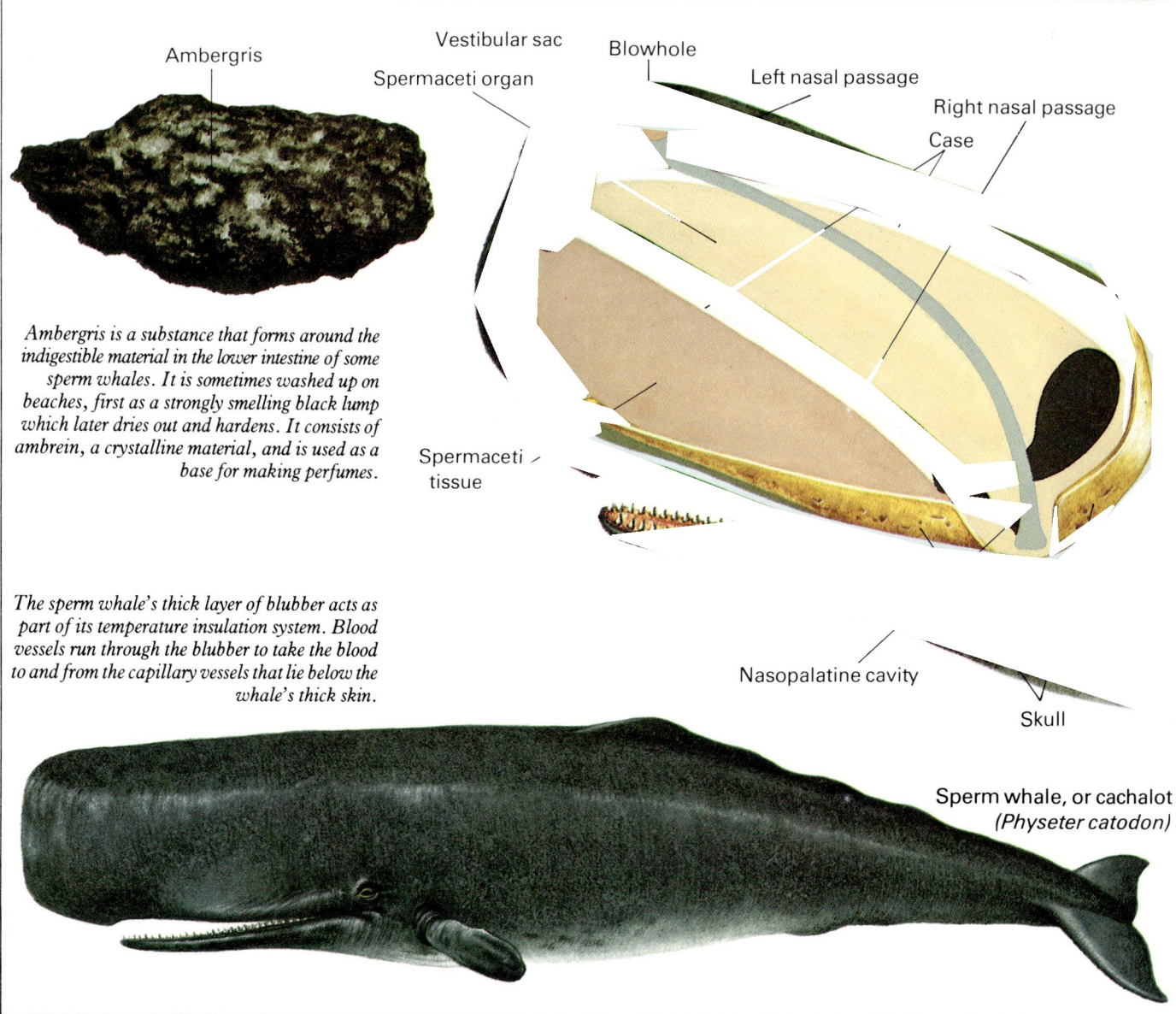

Ambergris

Vestibular sac
Spermaceti organ
Blowhole
Left nasal passage
Right nasal passage
Case

Spermaceti tissue

Ambergris is a substance that forms around the indigestible material in the lower intestine of some sperm whales. It is sometimes washed up on beaches, first as a strongly smelling black lump which later dries out and hardens. It consists of ambrein, a crystalline material, and is used as a base for making perfumes.

The sperm whale's thick layer of blubber acts as part of its temperature insulation system. Blood vessels run through the blubber to take the blood to and from the capillary vessels that lie below the whale's thick skin.

Nasopalatine cavity
Skull

Sperm whale, or cachalot
(Physeter catodon)

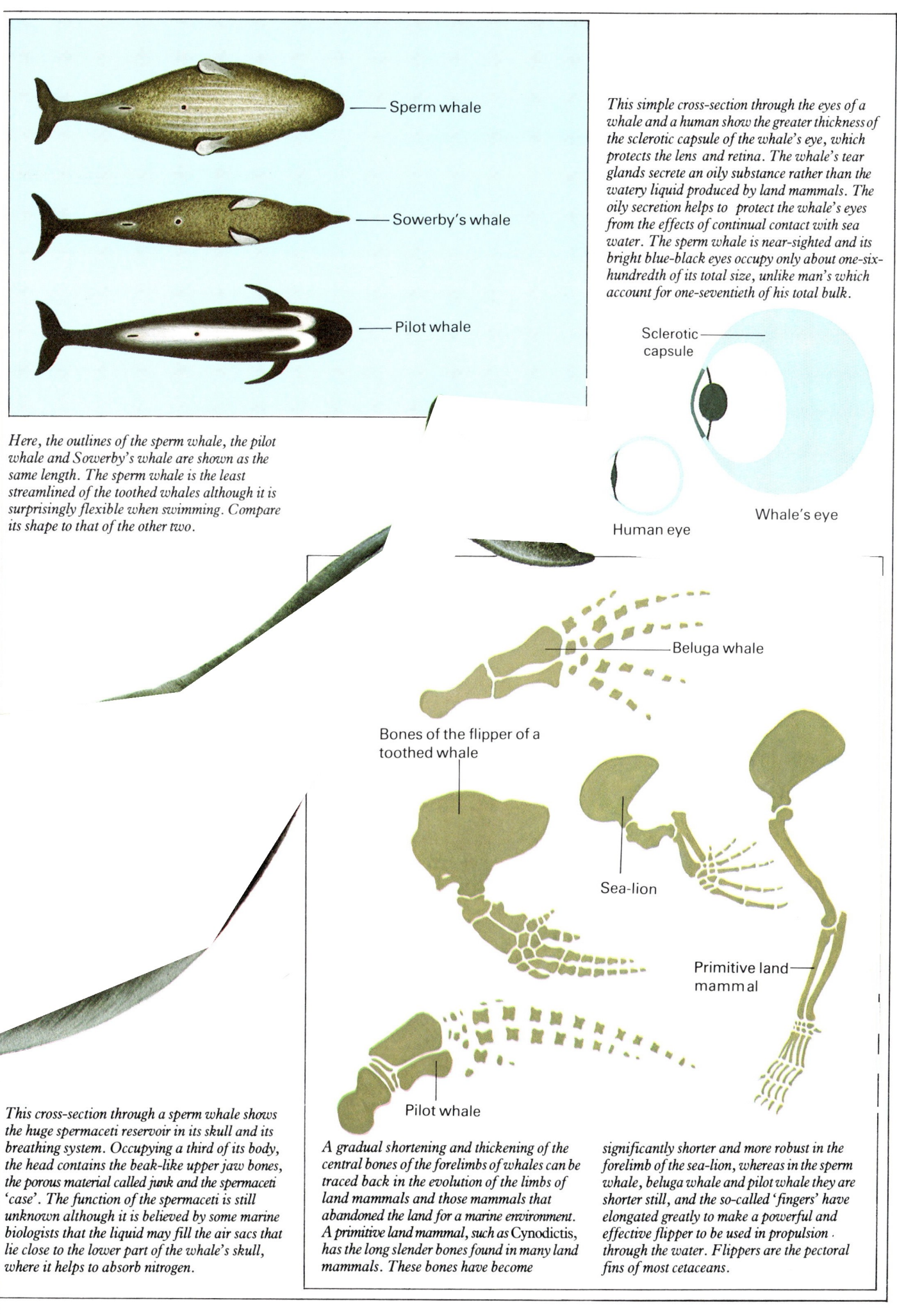

Sperm whale

Sowerby's whale

Pilot whale

Here, the outlines of the sperm whale, the pilot whale and Sowerby's whale are shown as the same length. The sperm whale is the least streamlined of the toothed whales although it is surprisingly flexible when swimming. Compare its shape to that of the other two.

This simple cross-section through the eyes of a whale and a human show the greater thickness of the sclerotic capsule of the whale's eye, which protects the lens and retina. The whale's tear glands secrete an oily substance rather than the watery liquid produced by land mammals. The oily secretion helps to protect the whale's eyes from the effects of continual contact with sea water. The sperm whale is near-sighted and its bright blue-black eyes occupy only about one-six-hundredth of its total size, unlike man's which account for one-seventieth of his total bulk.

Sclerotic capsule

Human eye

Whale's eye

Beluga whale

Bones of the flipper of a toothed whale

Sea-lion

Primitive land mammal

Pilot whale

This cross-section through a sperm whale shows the huge spermaceti reservoir in its skull and its breathing system. Occupying a third of its body, the head contains the beak-like upper jaw bones, the porous material called junk and the spermaceti 'case'. The function of the spermaceti is still unknown although it is believed by some marine biologists that the liquid may fill the air sacs that lie close to the lower part of the whale's skull, where it helps to absorb nitrogen.

A gradual shortening and thickening of the central bones of the forelimbs of whales can be traced back in the evolution of the limbs of land mammals and those mammals that abandoned the land for a marine environment. A primitive land mammal, such as Cynodictis, has the long slender bones found in many land mammals. These bones have become significantly shorter and more robust in the forelimb of the sea-lion, whereas in the sperm whale, beluga whale and pilot whale they are shorter still, and the so-called 'fingers' have elongated greatly to make a powerful and effective flipper to be used in propulsion through the water. Flippers are the pectoral fins of most cetaceans.

115

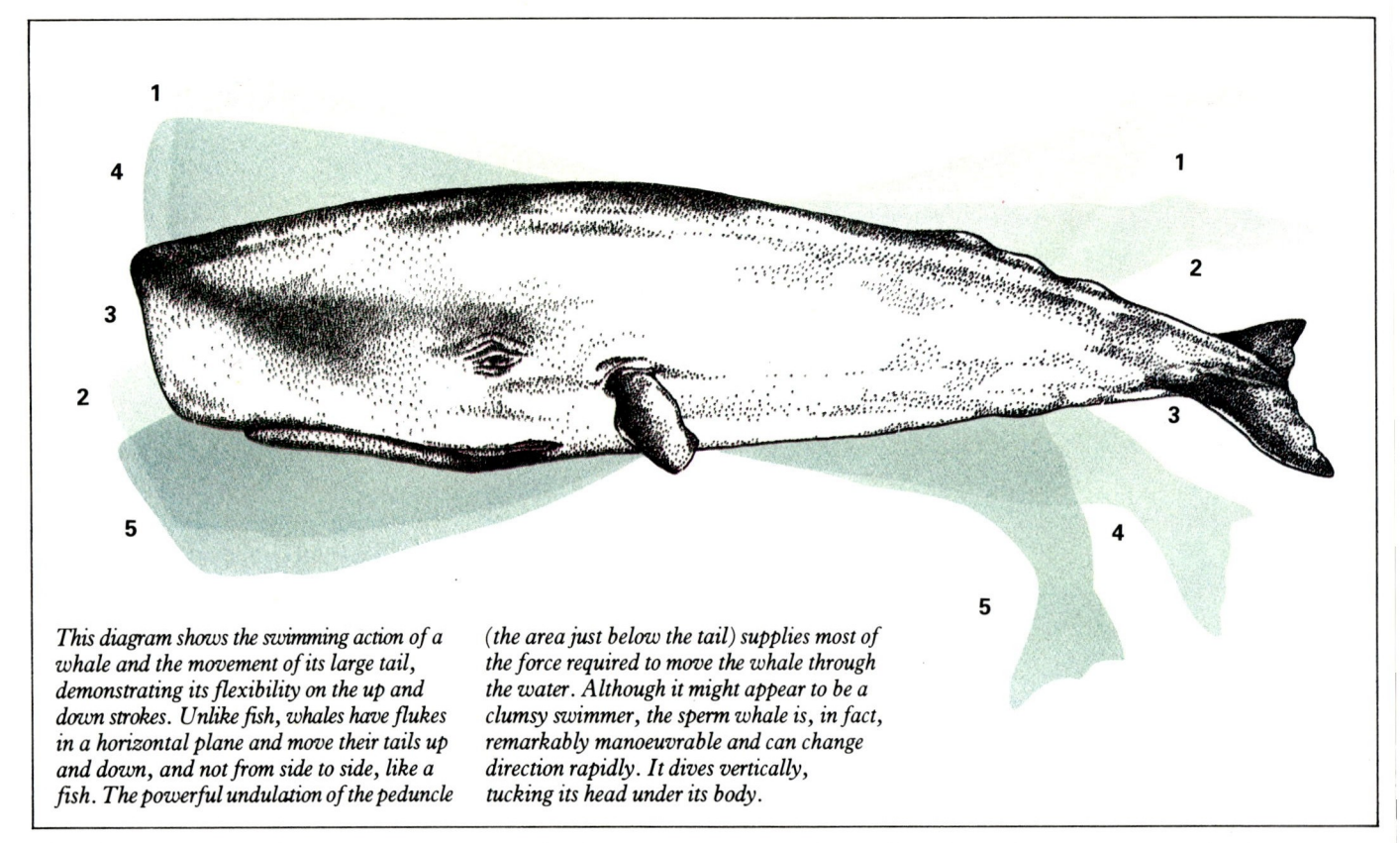

This diagram shows the swimming action of a whale and the movement of its large tail, demonstrating its flexibility on the up and down strokes. Unlike fish, whales have flukes in a horizontal plane and move their tails up and down, and not from side to side, like a fish. The powerful undulation of the peduncle (the area just below the tail) supplies most of the force required to move the whale through the water. Although it might appear to be a clumsy swimmer, the sperm whale is, in fact, remarkably manoeuvrable and can change direction rapidly. It dives vertically, tucking its head under its body.

The dive

A sperm whale can dive to great depths and swim there. It can also rise swiftly and surface without signs of the disastrous effects that such a sudden rise would produce in a human diver who descends to deep water and breathes air that is pumped to him at a high pressure. The nitrogen content of the air dissolves into his tissues and his blood. When he rises to the surface quickly, the nitrogen recovers its gaseous state in the form of minute bubbles. These block the circulation of blood to produce a state known variously as 'rapture of the deep', the 'bends' or 'caisson sickness': a form of gas embolism.

The whale escapes this danger by taking down with it its whole supply of air — not having the benefit of air pumps — and through a series of adaptive mechanisms that make it a natural diving animal.

In descending with all the air it needs for a dive, the whale carries only a small supply of nitrogen, and little of this is absorbed by the blood and tissues. The whale's body is not deformed under pressure, partly because it is about 90 per cent water, which is extremely hard to compress. However, the whale's lungs are compressed and their stock of air is forced into the windpipe and the air passage that lead to the blowhole. These passages are poorly supplied with blood vessels, so they absorb very little of the liquified nitrogen. The compression of the lungs makes their lining thicker, blocking off access to the capillaries, so, again, absorption of nitrogen is slight. The air passages and air sacs in the animal's head are filled with an emulsion of air, oil and water, and some scientists believe that the oil absorbs nitrogen. When the whale surfaces, it blows the emulsion through its blowhole with the used air.

Perhaps the most extraordinary accomplishment of the whale is that it can open its mouth without drowning at great depths. The convolutions of the whale's blowhole passage act as a valve to stop the escape of air and the invasion of the water. When the whale opens its mouth to catch its prey, the inner end of the blowhole passage, which projects into the windpipe, closes the windpipe so that the water cannot rush into the whale's lungs.

The sperm whale cannot supply the whole of its oxygen needs for a deep and long dive on the content of one breath of air alone. Much of its needs are supplied from air stored in air sacs and the oxygen in its muscles. A substance called myoglobin in the whale's muscle fibres retains large quantities of the oxygen that the whale uses during a dive.

While swimming under water, the whale's heart beat slows down drastically, saving oxygen but also making its distribution less efficient. Along the whale's spine and close to its brain are a series of finely branched arteries called *retia mirabilia*. This wonderful net of minute arteries operates to support the blood vessels with a reservoir of blood, or so it is believed. The function of the *retia mirabilia* is still not completely understood.

In a dive, the oxygen used by the sperm whale is stored in the lungs (9 per cent), the blood (41 per cent), the muscles (41 per cent) and in other tissues (9 per cent). This compares with the proportions of oxygen found in a human who makes an unassisted dive: lungs (34 per cent), blood (41 per cent), muscles (13 per cent) and in other tissues (12 per cent).

At a glance	
Sperm whale, or cachalot	
Physeter catodon	
Class	Mammalia
Order	Cetacea
Family	Physeteridae
Length	Male: up to 18.25m
	Female: up to 9.14m
Length of flippers	About 2m
Width of tail flukes	4-4.5m
Thickness of rubber	Up to 35.5cm
Body temperature	36°C, a little lower than most land mammals.
Weight	38-55 tonnes
Speed	Cruising 4-6 knots; sprinting 12 knots.
Lifespan	About 50 years.
Gestation period	12-16 months
Calf at birth	5m in length. It will grow at a rate of about 4.5 kg per hour on its mother's milk, which is approximately 35% richer than cow's milk.
Oil	A sperm whale will produce up to 30 barrels of oil and one tonne of spermaceti; a fine white waxy substance that whalers take from the sperm whale's massive head.

Sperm whale's skull

Seen from above, the skull of a sperm whale is wide and basin-shaped. It is the upper surface that holds the 'case' of spermaceti, a clear oil which solidifies on contact with cool air to form a waxy substance. The oil is stored in a lattice of tissues inside the bowl-shaped structure of the skull.

Unlike the upper jaw, the lower jaw is surprisingly narrow with two rows of undifferentiated teeth. Their function is to help the whale to seize its prey and hang on to it. Between 18 and 60 teeth line the rim of the lower jaw only and fit into slots in the upper jaw when the whale closes its enormous mouth.

Cross-section through backbone

Sperm whale's jaw

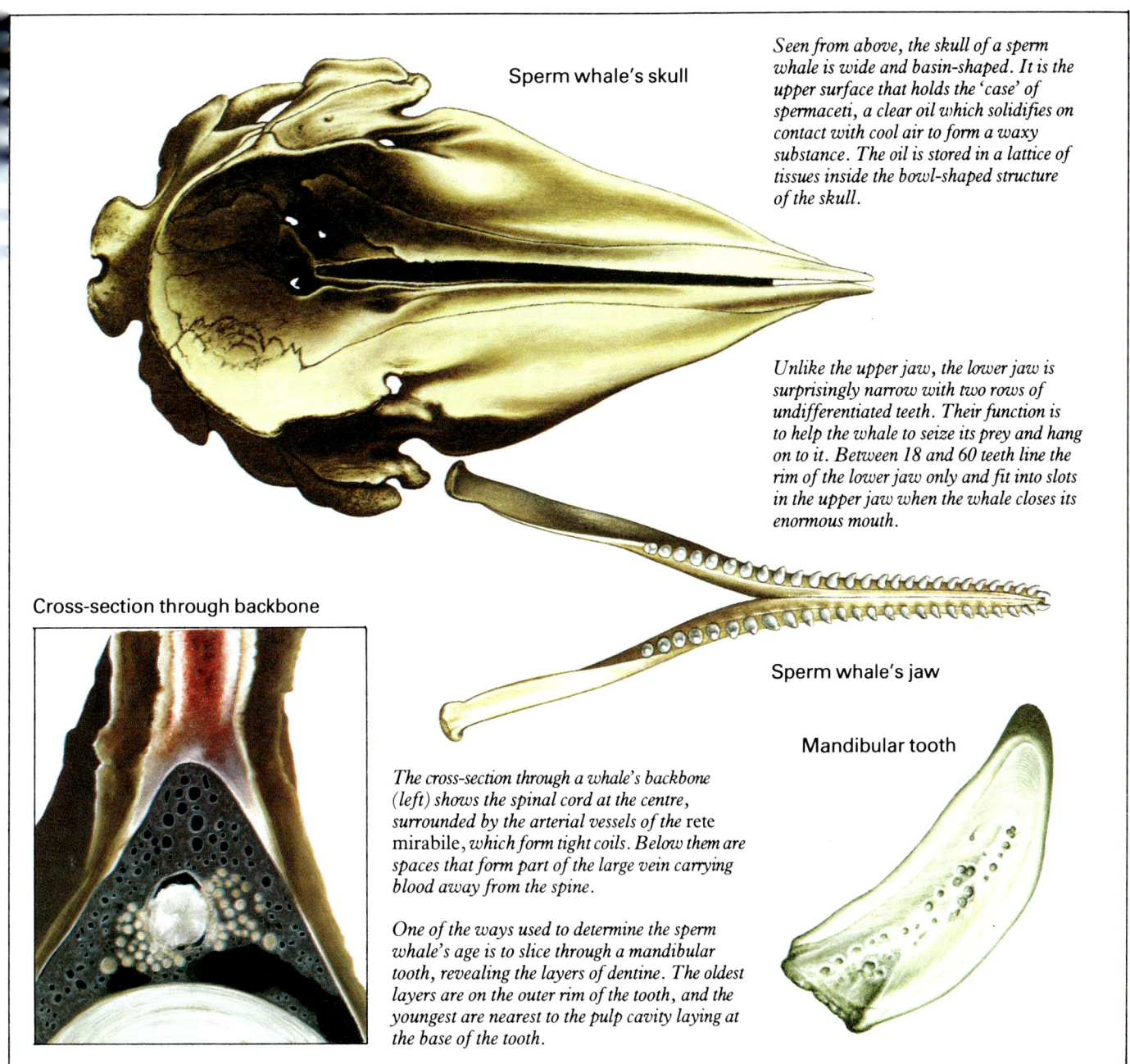

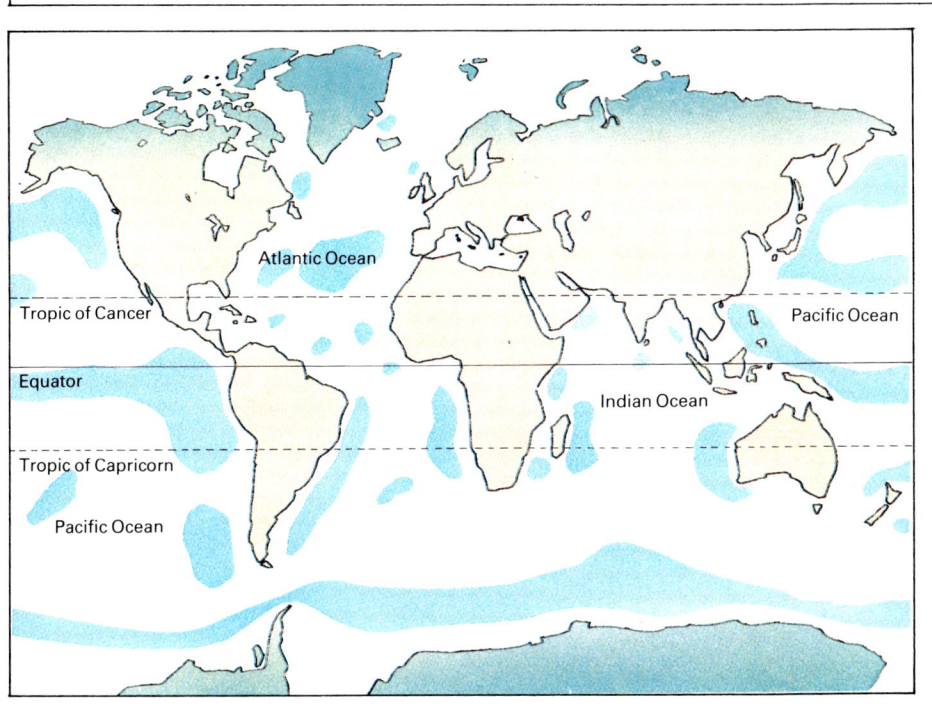

Mandibular tooth

The cross-section through a whale's backbone (left) shows the spinal cord at the centre, surrounded by the arterial vessels of the rete mirabile, which form tight coils. Below them are spaces that form part of the large vein carrying blood away from the spine.

One of the ways used to determine the sperm whale's age is to slice through a mandibular tooth, revealing the layers of dentine. The oldest layers are on the outer rim of the tooth, and the youngest are nearest to the pulp cavity laying at the base of the tooth.

This map shows the distribution of the sperm whale around the world. It is found in most of the world's oceans, ranging from the cold, polar Antarctic waters through the tropical and temperate seas of the Pacific, Atlantic and Indian oceans. The extent to which the stocks of sperm whales from these oceans mix is still uncertain, and marine biologists are trying to resolve this puzzle. However, the evidence suggests that the mixing is on a large scale. Sperm whales are still hunted extensively by whaling ships and the only restriction on their capture is one of length, factory ships being allowed to catch only those whales over 11.58m. This ruling serves to protect the female whales which rarely exceed 10.5m in length. If whalers adhere to these rules, concern over sperm whale stocks may be allayed for another decade or more. However, whaling activities are hard to monitor and the Scientific Committee of the International Whaling Commission has expressed serious doubts about the figures recorded by whalers.

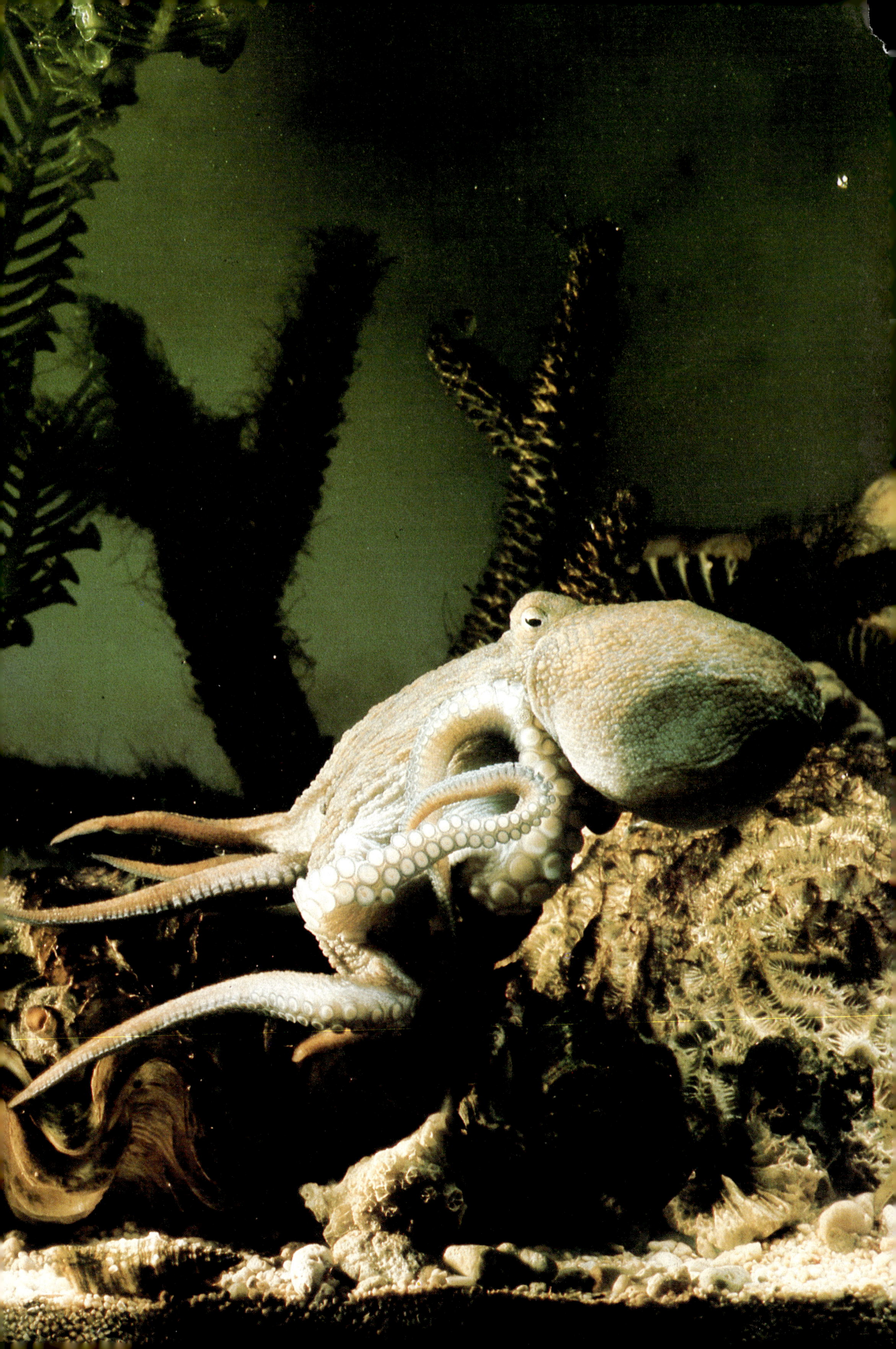

The Octopus

Low, slanting rays of a pale sun warmed a tumble of limestone boulders that, years before this evening, had crashed down the headland to the beach. Their jagged fractures had softened to a rounded smoothness over years of the ocean's pounding tides. Now, the sea lapped lightly against them, making soft sucking noises. Areas of paler rock appeared as the waves left them to dry in the sun's late light. A crab moved in its typical sideways motion across a smooth slope, its body raised clear of the rock. Water lapped a metre below the crab's lightly tapping claws. It paused in its journey, feelers waving and eyes swivelling, then it began to move diagonally away from the waves to its left towards a pool, thickly lined with seaweed.

A narrow stream of water curved through the air, catching sparks of light from the tawny sun. The water had risen from the sea itself and it landed with a splash, slightly upslope of the crab. The startled crustacean was bowled down the incline, struggling for a hold as the miniature torrent swept it over the edge of the rock and into the sea. The water dried slowly from the rock and that was the last the crab saw of dry land.

The crab sank slowly, tilting gently with the eddies of the tide, until it landed on a patch of pale sand. The creature was lifted slightly by a current of faintly discoloured water which enveloped its moving body. The crab's dash for cover halted abruptly and it sank down on its straddled legs until the base of its shell touched the sand. It lay still, its eyes glittering like small crystals.

After a few seconds, a long arm unfurled from a dark crevice in the rocks. It rippled towards the crab and touched it lightly. The crab did not move; the arm was withdrawn. From its narrow hiding-place emerged a male octopus flattening its body to slip between the rough sides of the rocky openings. Daintily, it picked its way over to its paralysed victim. Of its eight arms two became

Opposite page:
This common octopus is jetting over the sea-bed to pounce on an unsuspecting crab. Octopuses move either by walking on their arms across the bottom, or by jet propulsion, as shown here. This is achieved by expelling water through the funnel by means of contracting the mantle muscles. This form of locomotion is usually in a backwards direction, with arms close together streaming behind the body. Although jet propulsion is swift and allows an octopus to escape from potential predators, it is limited by the capacity of the mantle cavity to hold only a certain amount of water.

This octopus is eating a crab in its home in a triton shell. A carnivore, like other cephalopods, the octopus uses its large eyes to search for food. Crabs are often captured by shooting out a long arm and grasping the creature with its suckers. It soon becomes paralysed with the poisonous secretion of the posterior salivary glands. The octopus bites through the shell of the crab with its horny beak to separate it at the joints and remove the tissue. Digestion takes place mostly in the so-called 'liver' and the resulting waste matter is expelled.

The large, prominent eyes of the octopus are clearly visible on either side of its head as it lies in a cleft, waiting to snatch a passing crab with one of its long tentacles. It will remain motionless for long periods of time waiting until a prey creature approaches, spotting it with its keen eyesight. The mouth is at the centre of the bases of the arms, a circular lip surrounding the beak and the radula which are used to disjoint the prey and eat it.

legs as the octopus walked, spider-like, over the seafloor. Casually, the arms encircled the crab, drawing it towards the octopus's mouth. The sheering planes of the tough, horny beak moved apart and clamped on the edge of the crab's hard shell. A small hole was all that was necessary to allow the octopus to inject a liquid, similar to that which immobilised the crab. The enzymes in the fluid began softening the crab's tissues so that the octopus could later suck them from their protective shell.

The octopus did not complete his meal there and then. He drew the crab along with him until, after a short walk along the seabed, he arrived at a spot where two boulders formed an angle, resembling the sides of a half-opened book. In front of the open angle of these flat-sided boulders he had gathered together a cairn of stones that partially blocked the opening. Sliding past an open corner of his castle, he carried the crab inside and wedged it under one of the cairn stones. Above his head the sea's surface gleamed and changed as the water washed against the upper parts of the boulders rising out of the sea. The boulders formed the roof of the octopus's home. No predatory fish could catch him unawares through a roof like that. Any enemy would have to attack over the lip of the cairn of stones and the octopus concentrated his vigilance in that direction.

Curling a couple of arms around the secure base of one of the large boulders, the octopus swept out another arm and drew towards him a crab he had killed a little over a day ago. The movement stirred empty claw cases and shells from previous meals. His mouth protruded a little as he fed on the softened crab meat. All the time, his two great eyes peered through chinks in the walls of stones, fiercely alert for passing prey or predators. A small nursehound shark swam up to the octopus's castle but turned away with a sinuous twist of its body. The octopus paused in his eating but took no more than a passing interest in the fish; crab meat was more to his taste.

The pale light from the surface filtered down and the greenish-grey of the octopus seemed to absorb it subtly. His skin at times had the soft luminescent radiance of mother of pearl broken here and there by small reddish-brown protruberances. Delicate changes in the tone of his skin colours, so slight as to be barely perceptible, flowed constantly across his body. His arms waved gently, stirring the water about his 23cm body.

The summer light faded quite quickly. As darkness gathered in the water, the octopus became more active. He slid from his secure place and lightly stepped across the scatter of stones towards a sandy slope that led to deeper water. As he reached the rim of pebbles that marked the boundary of the sand, he passed a tilted slab of concrete. It lay half buried in the sand where it had fallen many years before when sea defences had been raised along the coast. From a hollow, excavated beneath it and protected by a wall of stones, the eyes of a large female looked listlessly out.

In the spring he had found her and mated with her. He had approached her with caution, his skin glowing with changing colour. He had waved his arms, presenting clearly to her the largest of his suckers at the base of his second pair of arms. At first she had turned her funnel towards him and jetted away but he was persistent. Swimming after her, he had waited until she rested and then he had unwound his third arm and reached out to her. This arm had changed as he had become sexually mature and as the mating season had arrived. It was not like his other arms but had grown longer with a furrowed spoon-shaped pad at the tip. He had caressed the female with his mating arm, gently trying to slip it under her mantle

The soft body of the octopus is particularly vulnerable to predators, especially when it is away from the protection of its home in a shell or a rock. The octopus adopts a defensive posture when attacked and exposes its suckers to its enemy. Its most effective protective device, however, is its capacity to squirt a dark cloud of ink, containing melanin, at an attacker. It can then escape backwards behind the black suspension formed in the water by the ink.

This venomous blue ring octopus is camouflaged against the pebbles and stones of the sea-bed. Many octopuses can change their colour, outline, skin texture and even body form itself to blend into their surroundings and escape detection by predators or prey. The chromatophores, between one and two million cells containing pigments in the octopus's body, cause these colour changes. Controlled by the brain, the dark and light pigment-containing chromatophores have an expandible wall with radial muslces. Their activity is monitored by the nervous system.

but she had shrugged away from him. Slowly following her, he had encouraged her with his stroking arm, always keeping his body at a discreet distance. Little by little she had settled down under his courtship and allowed him to insert his mating arm under the rim of her mantle. Once it was in position there had been a pause before small packets of sperms had flowed down the grooves of his altered arm into the female, fertilising her eggs. For more than two hours they mated, sitting nearly a metre apart, colours blushing across their bodies in waves of russet brown.

When the mating had ended, she had swum away to her lair and he had taken little further interest in her. Her work had just begun. She had minutely cleaned every part of her den, hosing it with water squirted through her funnel and wiping clear all food debris that might decay.

She had laid her eggs over a period of a fortnight. As each cluster of eggs emerged she had glued it to the roof of her cave under the concrete block. At the end of the laying she had 48 clusters, each of about 1000 eggs. The clusters hung from her roof like bunches of bananas, each 'banana' about the size of a grain of rice. She had never rested from her care for the eggs. She gently blew oxygen-rich water over them from her funnel, caressing them with her arms to brush away any parasites that might make their home among her brood. She had cared for the eggs for nearly five weeks – in warmer waters she might have seen them hatch in four – before the minute young had appeared. They struggled from the security of the eggs and swam about the cave. There was a cloud of them, each being no more than the size of a flea. As the thousands of baby octopuses had left the cave and moved towards the light to join the plankton, shoals of mullet had swam among them, snapping up several at a time. The female octopus in her cave had continued to stroke and fondle the skins of the eggs that festooned her home.

All the time she had cared for her eggs she had eaten barely anything. Now that the young had gone, she ate nothing. By the time the male walked and swam past her cave on his way to the deep water, she had eaten parts of two of her own arms and had not got much longer to live.

As the male octopus crossed the sandy slope, a thornback ray flicked up puffs of sand with the extremities of its flat body, anxious to keep out of the octopus's reach. Bounding upwards to avoid a tangle of debris, the octopus, which had no interest in the ray, drew water into himself by expanding the walls of his mantle. The water entered round the free edge at his neck. The inlet closed, ridges of cartilage locked to form a seal in the depressions around the sides of the funnel and his head retracted towards his pouch-like body.

This large, spotted moray eel is looming out of an underwater rocky cavity beside a shoal of grunts. One of the octopus's most important predators, the moray eel is an inhabitant of warm and tropical seas. It is also found in the Mediterranean. Large and naked with a mottled body, this huge eel often lives in holes in rocks and coral and has a voracious appetite. It may reach up to four metres in length, and its size and sharp, biting teeth make it a formidable opponent of the octopus.

123

The embryo is visible in this view of the common octopus's egg. Mating takes place in the spring close to the shore, the male using his third arm to deposit the spermatophores in the female's mantal cavity. Between 50,000 and 180,000 eggs are laid in long strings. The female attaches them to rocks and guards them over the three to nine week period before they hatch. During this time, she eats nothing and dies when the larvae hatch from the eggs. The newly born larvae swim up to the sea's surface and float there in the ocean currents for one to three months before settling on the sea-bed to develop and grow further.

When the water was sealed in, his mantle contracted and drove the water out through his funnel to force him backwards.

He was an agile swimmer; small adjustments to the angle of his funnel, assisted by flicks of his arms, moved him in any direction he wanted. In the dark water, he was conscious of currents and the presence of fish around him. Although his eyes were not of much value in these conditions, the chemical receptors that covered his body sent a continuous pattern of messages to his brain informing him of his surroundings.

Late at night, he settled halfway into a crevice that formed part of a small rift in the seafloor. Here he was lucky enough to encounter one of his most favoured foods – lobster. He had lain in wait for just such a possibility, blending perfectly with his surroundings, a shapeless mass against the rock. The lobster was of a good size. It moved slowly and confidently past the octopus, whose first two pairs of arms hovered above the crustacean while another slipped very gently behind it. With a flurry, the octopus ensnared his prey. The lobster fought but the octopus was certain of success when he tore off one of his opponent's claws. The octopus's black beak cracked into the lobster's thick carapace and the battle ended as the crustacean collapsed, paralysed by the enzymes now working on its tissue and nervous system.

The sun was searching the depths as the octopus made his way towards the tangle of debris he had passed in the darkness. He was moving slowly, carrying parts of the lobster he had caught earlier.

He directed his funnel downwards and jetted clear of the obstacle. A few metres below, a smooth, blunt head twitched as if with hungry anticipation. The octopus was aware of the moray eel as soon as she shot from the discarded piping in which she had made her home. Her two-metre body snaking through the water was thick with muscle. She was certain to catch the octopus in a few seconds, despite the sudden surge of speed the octopus produced. He dropped his prize and blanched an ashy-white as he released a cloud of ink between himself and the pursuing eel.

For a moment the octopus seemed to have fooled the eel, which paused, poking her nose towards the ink cloud. The octopus had banked sharply and his pale colouration made him hard to see. The eel suddenly spotted him against the pale, glistening undersurface of the sea and shot after him. Once again, the octopus released a puff of ink and changed course in the hope that the phantom image left by the dark purple stain would distract the eel but she was too far away and saw the change of direction. She darted and seized the octopus by an arm, twisting and wrenching at it. The octopus fought furiously to free himself from the eel's sharp teeth and succeeded in reducing her twisting action by enmeshing the long body in his free arms but he could not bring his powerful beak to bear effectively on her. The struggle was deadly and the eel's teeth bit deeper. Then, quite suddenly, it was over. The octopus was free. His arm was severed a little above the eel's teeth and the eel was enveloped by a cloud of ink. The arm had been bitten through: it had been jettisoned by the octopus in the interests of survival. The eel dropped the arm and twisted clear of the ink, which clearly repelled her. Not even bothering to retrieve the arm, the eel swam back to her lair.

The octopus reached his home and settled inside. The stump of the arm would soon skin over and a replacement arm would grow slowly. In the meantime, he would survive quite well with seven. Above his head, the octopus watched his roof silver over with the light of a noonday sun.

This close-up view of the octopus's suckers shows their structure. There are two rows of suckers on each of the octopus's eight arms, each of which has tiny hooks around its rim for gripping slippery prey and drawing it up to the octopus's mouth. The deeply set, fleshy suckers contain receptors which are sufficiently sensitive to distinguish between the nature of different animals and objects and to transmit this information directly to the brain.

The cephalopods

Cephalopods inhabit all the oceans of the world in many forms, from the beautifully symmetrical small nautilus to the shapeless Pacific octopus (*Paroctopus apollyon*). The variety of guises in which this class of animal has evolved reflects a remarkable capacity of adaptation to its environment.

Some people might wonder why, in their long and successful history, the cephalopods have not emerged from the oceans to colonise dry land; the animals' nervous and digestive systems and their limbs might easily have adapted to a new environment. The solution to the problem might be found in the constitution of the cephalopod's blood. The blood pigment is not the haemoglobin found in land animals and many fish, but haemocyanin — a copper pigment of a blue colour. The pigment is a poor carrier of the compared to 10-20 per 100 carried by the blood of fish that have haemoglobin. This means that a cephalopod lives closer to its physical limits than a similarly active vertebrate animals. Cephalopod blood carries 3.1-4.5 volumes of oxygen per 100 volumes and probably could not make the drastic adaptive journey from ocean waters, where oxygen levels are more constant than in most freshwater environments, to rivers, lakes and swamps, and eventually to dry land.

Hunters of the seas

Cephalopods are probably the most feared of all invertebrate hunters. Members of the group of animals that have no backbones, the cephalopods are wonderfully adapted to their ocean environment. Of the 650 or so species of the class that are identified today, about 170 species belong to the order *Octopoda*, which divides into two suborders: *Cirrat* and *Incirrata*. The *Incirrata* are what most people know as octopuses in our oceans today.

Octopuses vary greatly in size. The smallest is *Octopus arborescens*, which measures no more than 51mm across — a minute fraction of the size of its giant relative, *O. hongkongensis*, which has been found with an armspan of over nine metres. Octopuses rarely live more than one-and-a-half kilometres below the surface, but of life below these depths marine biologists know little, and their theories are often contradicted by totally new discoveries. *Stauroteuthidae grimpoteuthis*, a species of the suborder *Cirrata*, became entangled in a trawl at the astonishing depth of 13.30km in the Weddell Sea. Octopuses that live at these depths are generally jelly-like creatures whose structures are almost transparent. Their tissues are filled with fluid, and this watery substance is virtually incompressible, leaving the octopus little affected by the pressure of the surrounding water. *S. grimpoteuthis* must have been resisting a pressure of nearly three tonnes per square centimetre when at this depth.

The octopus's very curious appearance, its bizarre arrangement of multiple arms, huge eyes and, in some species, its great size, have fueled the imagination of maritime storytellers for many years. While the Disneyesque tales of giant octopuses dragging liners to their doom cannot be credited, there are accounts of small ships that seem to have succumbed to

At a glance
Common octopus
Octopus vulgaris

Phylum	Mollusca
Class	Cephalopoda
Order	Octopoda
Family	Octopodiae
Span of arms	Up to 3m in large Mediterranean specimens, but the largest caught in British waters was 1.83m and weighed 3.30kg.
Weight	Male: 8-10kg (an exceptional 25kg has been reported) Female: 6-7kg
Maximum depth	About 400m
Swimming speed	6.5km/h when migrating but up to 13km/h when escaping from attack.
Speed on land	About 7km/h when hurrying.
Egg	3.17mm long, translucent in appearance.
Eggs	Laid in clusters; 5,000 may be laid by one female in a fortnight.
Incubation period	4-5 weeks for the eggs.
Lifespan	About 8 years maximum.

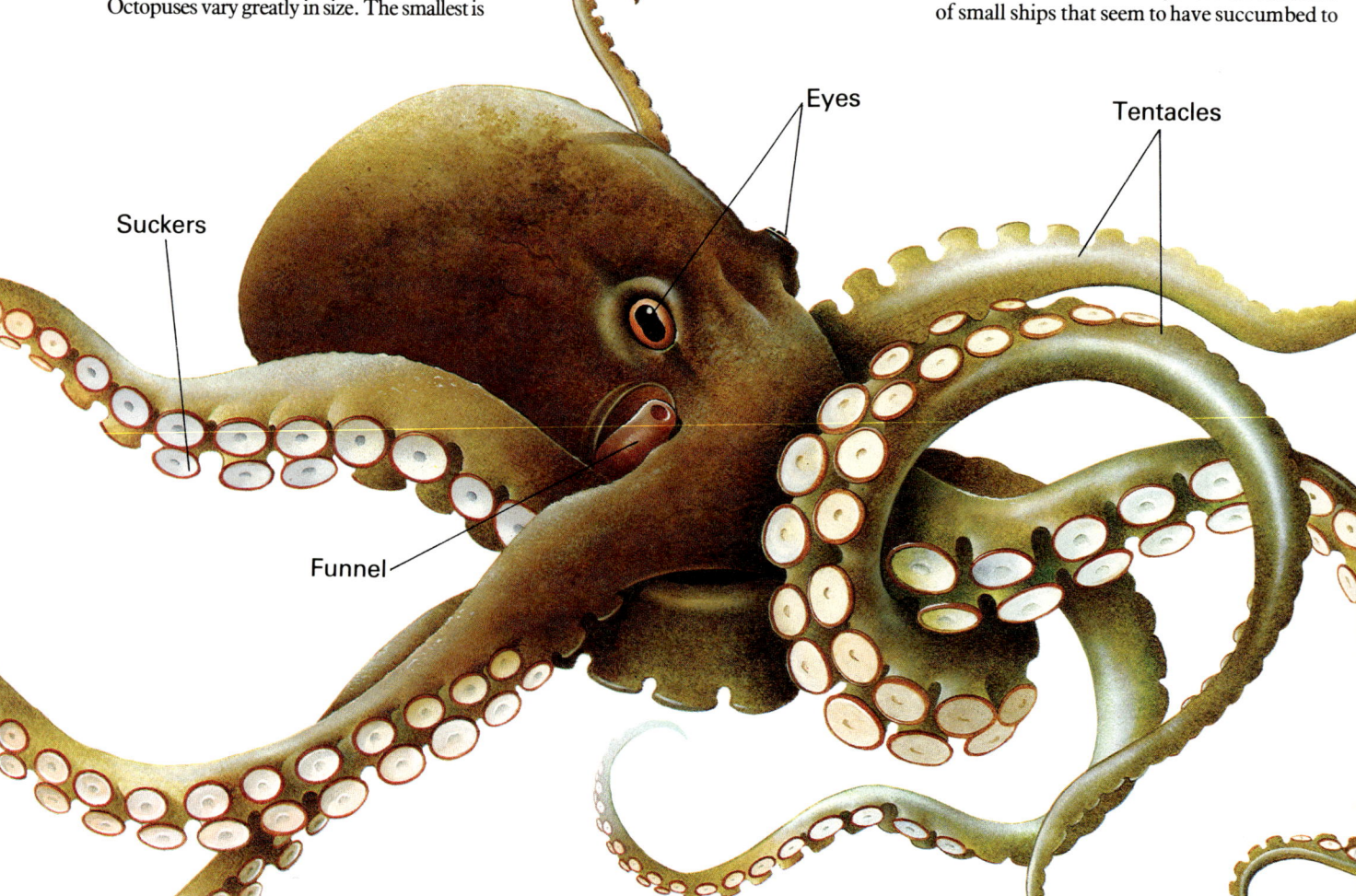

the assaults of sea creatures which must have resembled the shy octopus. In these tales, there is a noticeable confusion about the type of creature attacking a vessel: calumary, squid cuttlefish and kraken are some of the names that have been used to describe them, but they were likely to have been giant squids of the genus Architeuthis, larger species of which may reach nearly 15m from the tips of their tentacles to the points of their tails.

The miraculous octopus

What stranger creature is there than one that changes its colour in a split second, has eight arms which it can shed and grow again at will, a pair of huge goggle eyes, can eat a lobster without cracking it open, has the strength to hold a diver clamped to a rock, and swims by jet propulsion? It would be easy to list other strange attributes of the octopus, but these few make it easy to see why this creature grips our imagination. There is a great deal to be learned about this animal: its life is still, in many respects, secret, and the only species that has been studied to an advanced degree is the common octopus, but much remains of even that octopus's mystery.

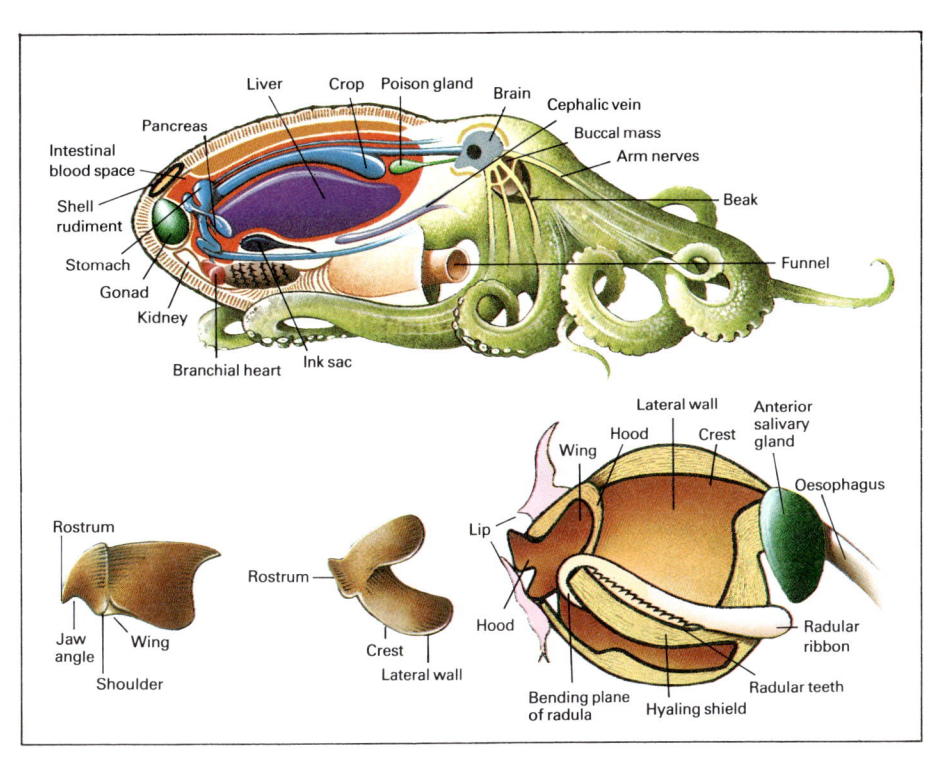

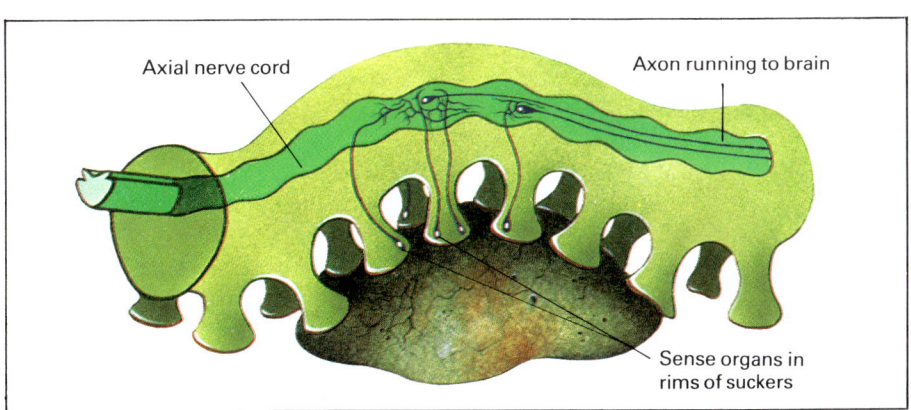

The internal organs of the octopus and the relationship between the beak, radula and other parts of the body are illustrated (above). The sense organs in the rims of the suckers are also shown (left). The suckers, which run in a double row along each arm, are delicate sensors as well as mechanical devices to aid the creature in its movements and quest for food. The suckers can detect irregularities in the surface of an object by means of the sensors. The sense organs supply part of the axial cord with information about an object which is then transmitted to the brain of the octopus so that it can identify strange objects.

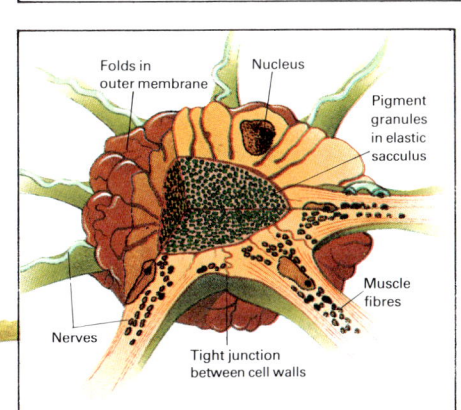

This cross-section shows an octopus's chromaphore with its muscles relaxed. The chromatophore is a pigment-containing cell which enables the octopus to change colour and to camouflage itself against its surroundings. Some chromatophores are lighter than others, having a white centre.

The body of the octopus lacks a skeleton so that it can squeeze through narrow spaces and holes. The animal's organs lie within a tough mantle and include a pair of gills whereby it extracts oxygen and nutrients from sea water, a pair of kidneys and three hearts for pumping blood around the body.

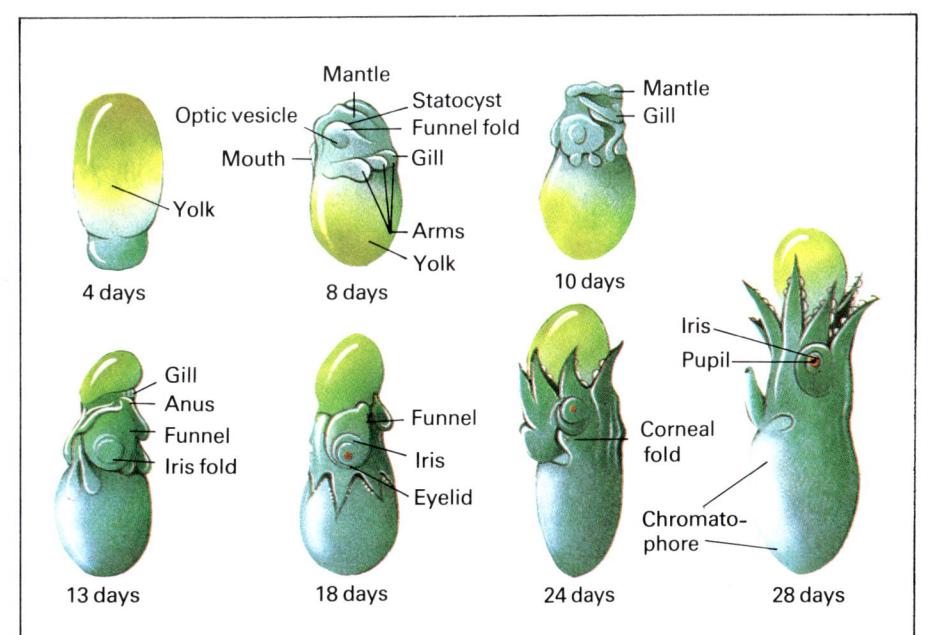

The stages in the development of the embryo of Octopus vulgaris are shown above from four days after spawning when the ectoderm begins to spread down over the yolk and rudimentary arms, eyes, mantle and funnel start to appear. These and the internal organs continue to develop inside the embryo as the yolk sac reduces in size and the animal prepares to hatch. The animal turns round in the egg prior to hatching and a special gland forms at the mantle's end which weakens the egg shell so that the octopus can emerge.

127

Picture Credits

Heather Angel
pages 38,41,53,55,123
Ardea
pages 14,70,74,75,82
Bay Picture Library
pages 20,23,50,57,84,125
J. Allen Cash
endpapers
Bruce Coleman
pages 30,36-37,48,51,52,124
Colour Library International
contents page and introductory page
Pat Morris
pages 77,111
Natural History Photographic Agency
cover, half-title page and pages 55,63,64,76,93,96
Naturfoto
pages 16,32,58,60,61,62,87,95,118,119,121
Nature Photographers
pages 19,85,109
Picturepoint
pages 94,122
Popperfoto
page 55
Satour
page 18
Seaphot/Christian Petron
pages 72-73,104-105
Tony Stone Associates
pages 12-13
Survival Anglia
pages 10,17,40,42,43,106,107,108
Zefa Picture Library
pages 15,25,31,45,65,77,78,86,97,101,110,111,120

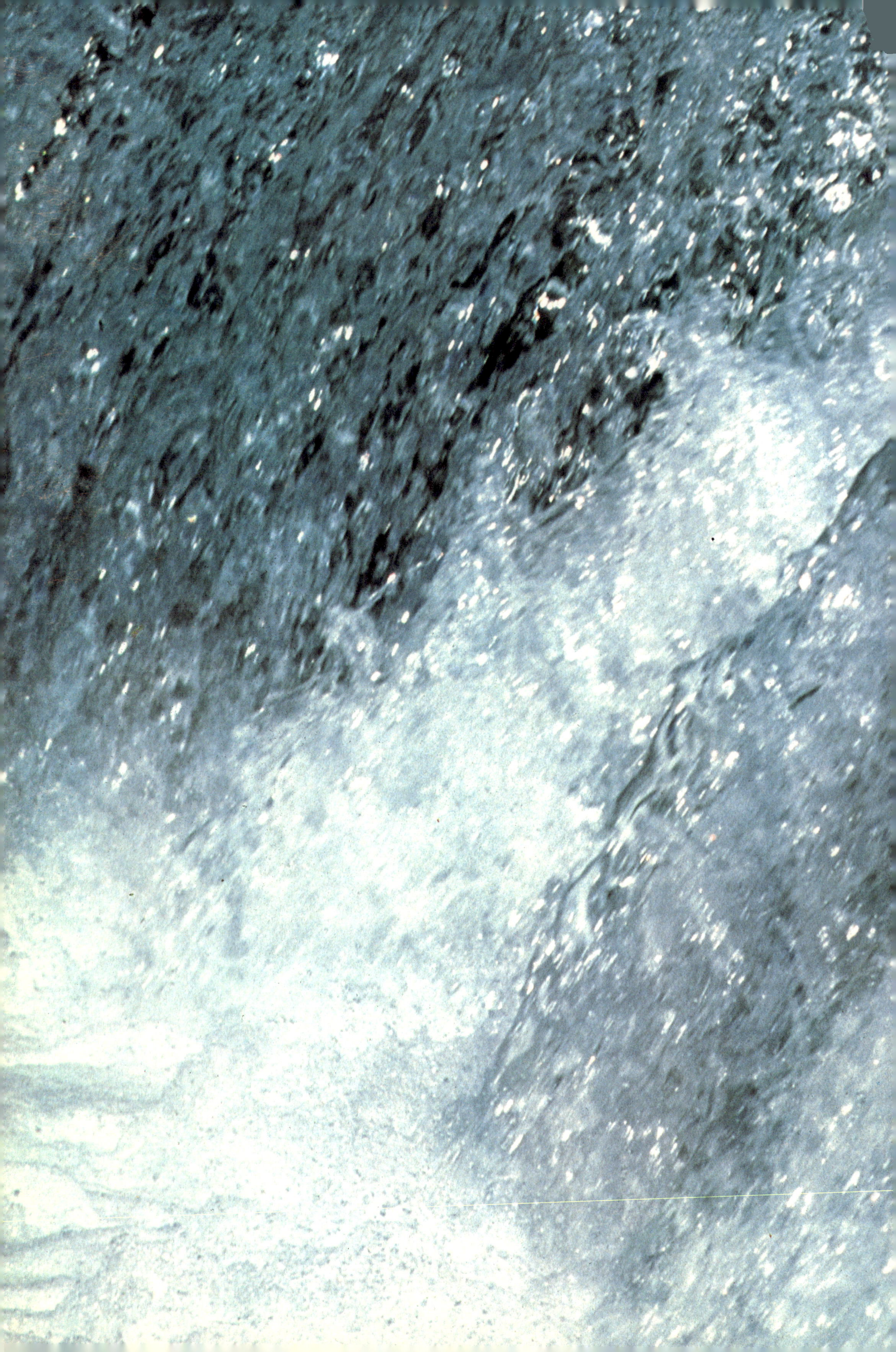